I0440906

U.S. Fish & Wildlife Service

Informing Ecosystem Management: Science and Process for Landbird Conservation in the Western United States

Biological Technical Publication
BTP-R1014-2011

Jaime L. Stephens[1]

Kimberly Kreitinger[2]

C. John Ralph[3]

Michael T. Green[4]

[1] Klamath Bird Observatory, Ashland, OR
[2] PRBO Conservation Science, Petaluma, CA
[3] U.S.D.A. Forest Service, Redwood Sciences Laboratory, Arcata, CA
[4] U.S. Fish and Wildlife Service, Portland, OR

Photo credit: © Jim Livaudais

Cover Design: From Nyberg (1999)

Cover birds, clockwise from top: Bell's Vireo (*Vireo bellii*), Black-throated Gray Warbler (*Dendroica nigrescens*), Nashville Warbler (*Vermivora ruficapilla*), Purple Finch (*Carpodacus purpureus*), Winter Wren (*Troglodytes troglodytes*), Yellow-breasted Chat (*Icteria virens*)

Editor Contact Information:

Jaime L. Stephens
Klamath Bird Observatory
P.O. Box 758
Ashland, OR 97520
Phone: (541) 282-0866
E-mail: jlh@klamathbird.org

Kimberly Kreitinger
PRBO Conservation Science
3820 Cypress Drive #11
Petaluma, CA 94954
Phone: (415) 265-9153
E-mail: K.Kreitinger@gmail.com

C. John Ralph
USFS Redwood Sciences Laboratory
1700 Bayview Drive
Arcata, CA 95521
Phone: (707) 825-2992
E-mail: cjralph@humboldt1.com

Michael T. Green
U.S. Fish and Wildlife Service
Division of Migratory Birds and Habitat Programs
911 Northeast 11th Ave
Portland, OR 97232
Phone: (503) 872-2707
E-mail: Michael_Green@fws.gov

For additional copies or information, contact:

Jaime L. Stephens
Klamath Bird Observatory
P.O. Box 758
Ashland, OR 97520
Phone: (541) 282-0866
E-mail: jlh@klamathbird.org

Recommended Citation:

Stephens, J. L., K. Kreitinger, C. J. Ralph, and M. T. Green (editors). 2011. Informing ecosystem management: science and process for landbird conservation in the western United States. U.S. Department of Interior, Fish and Wildlife Service, Biological Technical Publication, FWS/ BTP-R1014-2011, Washington, D.C.

Series Technical Editor:

Stephanie L. Jones
U.S. Fish and Wildlife Service
Nongame Migratory Bird Coordinator
P.O. Box 25486
Denver Federal Center
Denver, CO 80225-0486

Table of Contents

Preface

Jaime L. Stephens, Kimberly Kreitinger, C. John Ralph, and Michael T. Green

Integrating bird conservation with land management

Recent advances in bird conservation are marked by the integration of science and land management. Information gained from past research can now be used to develop user-friendly management tools. Partners in Flight (Rich et al. 2004) as well as shorebirds (Brown et al. 2001), waterbirds (Kushlan et al. 2002), and especially waterfowl (North American Waterfowl Management Plan Committee 2004) initiatives use their respective conservation plans to catalyze this process and influence land management planning across the landscape. Using these conservation plans within a broader monitoring framework, managers can glean pertinent information about ecosystem dynamics.

Why monitor birds?

Land managers work in a setting where change is continuous and unpredictable (Bosch et al. 2003). Within this dynamic environment, they often are faced with making management decisions without any scientific support to guide them. Management activities need to be linked to the scientific process in order to better understand potential influences on the surrounding ecosystem. One scientific tool that will help to forge this link is monitoring. Monitoring measures population and habitat change and often elucidates the causes of change. Performed in concert with management actions, monitoring can help to evaluate the effectiveness of management prescriptions (Alexander et al. 2007) and provide assurance that management efforts are focusing on agreed-upon goals (Keough and Blahna 2006).

Land managers and biologists commonly monitor birds, both to track bird populations themselves, and as a tool to measure ecosystem health as a whole. Birds are relatively easy and cost-effective to monitor and standardized methodologies exist to allow comparisons across sites (Ralph et al. 1993). Birds occupy a wide diversity of ecological niches and respond quickly to changes in their environment. While bird monitoring is common, it is not always clear exactly what is gained by this monitoring. Primarily, bird monitoring is integral in answering the immediate questions about the effects of land management on an ecosystem. In addition, the value of monitoring data could increase with time as it contributes to answering longer and larger scale questions. However, monitoring data are only as valuable as the extent to which they are applied.

It is therefore important that we step back and evaluate the influence that bird monitoring projects have had on management. With this, we can learn from the past and inform others of how to implement successful, meaningful monitoring projects for the future.

How do adaptive management and monitoring interact?

This volume highlights bird conservation successes resulting from the integration of science, management, and learning within a collaborative framework, i.e., adaptive management (Jacobson et al. 2006). The adaptive management process consists of six stages: assessment, design, implementation, monitoring, evaluation, and adjustment. Land management projects are implemented one stage at a time and tested at each step, allowing for detection and correction of any deleterious effects (Moir and Block 2001). Ideally, information from one stage is incorporated into subsequent stages and an informational feedback loop or "adaptive management circle" is created. When properly integrated, the process is continuous, cyclic, and constantly evolving (Haney and Power 1996).

Examples from the western United States

In this publication, we present ten examples illustrating both the process and science behind bird conservation throughout the western United States. We begin with a series of papers that describe integrating bird conservation and effectiveness monitoring into land management guidelines and emphasize the importance of partnerships. This is followed by a series of case studies which highlight bird monitoring within the adaptive management framework. We emphasize the science of monitoring and the process of its integration into land management because both are necessary in order for effectiveness monitoring to fully impact decision making.

Acknowledgments

We thank John D. Alexander, Bob Altman, Barb Bresson, Geoff R. Geupel, Aaron L. Holmes, Melissa Pitkin, and Terry D. Rich who were integral in the workshop that was the inspiration for this publication, *"Tools for Bird Conservation in Conifer Forests: A Joint California and Oregon-Washington Partners in Flight Workshop,"* held in

Ashland Oregon in April 2005. Many thanks to Bob Altman, Carol J. Beardmore, Joe Buchanan, Ryan D. Burnett, Barb Bresson, Dan Casey, David Craig, Joe Fontaine, Thomas Gardali, Joan C. Hagar, Rob Holbrook, Gary Ivey, Dave Mauser, Larry Neel, Nadav Nur, Arvand O. Panjabi, Scott F. Pearson, Hildy Reiser, Jon Robinson, Christopher Rustay, Steve I. Rothstein, Paul Roush, Nathaniel E. Seavy, Tom Will, Julian K. Wood, and Jock Young for their review of these papers. We would also like to thank Danielle M. Morris for her assistance with editing and formatting the compiled works. In addition, we are grateful to the authors for their contribution to this publication. Partial funding for this publication was granted by the National Fish and Wildlife Foundation, the M. J. Murdock Charitable Trust, and U.S. Fish and Wildlife Service, Region 1, Division of Migratory Birds and Habitat Programs.

Integrating Partners in Flight Bird Conservation and Priority Land Management Objectives

John D. Alexander

Abstract

Using results from ongoing research and monitoring studies in the Klamath-Siskiyou Region of northern California and southern Oregon, I demonstrate how a Partners in Flight conservation planning strategy can be implemented using an adaptive management approach. Partners in Flight's planning strategy involves: 1) species and habitat assessment to derive population and habitat objectives for focal species; 2) working with land managers to integrate these objectives into management plans and implementing conservation actions on the ground; and 3) monitoring the effectiveness of these actions as an evaluation component of the conservation strategy. These conservation strategy components allow land managers to design projects that simultaneously meet priority management objectives (e.g., fire hazard reduction) and achieve bird conservation objectives. Monitoring bird community response to such projects leads to refinements or adaptations to future management actions, a critical step for managers concerned with achieving certain desired conditions within an adaptive management framework.

Introduction

Partners in Flight (PIF) has developed a conservation planning strategy (Bonney et al. 1999) that serves as a model for integrating bird conservation objectives into land management programs through the adaptive management framework (Fig. 1; Nyberg 1999). This strategy involves: 1) assessing the conservation status of bird species at continental and regional scales; 2) identifying habitat characteristics important for species of concern; 3) implementing land management actions that improve habitat characteristics for those species; and 4) monitoring the response of those species to evaluate the effectiveness of management actions.

Adaptive management is a systematic approach for improving resource management by learning from management outcomes (Williams et al. 2009). It has been traditionally conceptualized as a circular feedback loop with six components (Fig. 1). Working through this framework land managers: 1) assess

issues and develop management objectives; 2) design management actions to achieve objectives (e.g., desired conditions); 3) implement management actions; 4) monitor the results of management actions; 5) use monitoring results to evaluate the efficacy of the management actions in achieving the objectives; and 6) adjust treatments, prescriptions, plans, and policies accordingly.

PIF's conservation planning strategy is a process that uses science-based information about birds to link bird conservation objectives and management issues. Using results from research and monitoring efforts in the Klamath-Siskiyou Region, I demonstrate how PIF's conservation planning strategy can be implemented within the adaptive management framework to integrate bird conservation objectives with priority land management challenges.

Assessing populations and designing conservation objectives

Bird conservation plans present a synthesis of priorities and objectives to guide landbird conservation actions (Rich et al. 2004). To design and implement meaningful bird conservation plans, conservation issues must be assessed at multiple scales. Traditional conservation efforts based on a single-species approach, often driven by the

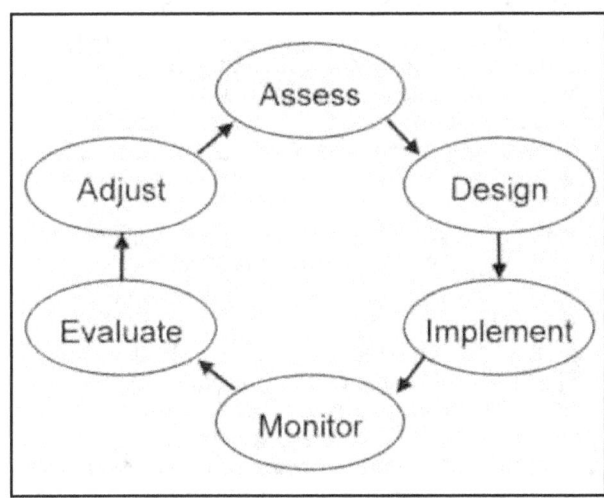

Figure 1. The traditional circular model of the adaptive management framework from Nyberg (1999).

Endangered Species Act (Endangered Species Act 1973; ESA), are not adequate for addressing continent-wide bird population declines (Bonney et al. 1999). The PIF approach to proactive conservation considers a suite of focal species (Chase and Geupel 2005) with the ultimate goal of reversing population declines before ESA listing becomes necessary (Rich et al. 2004).

A continental assessment of all landbirds was completed in 2004 (Rich et al. 2004). Population trends generated from the Breeding Bird Survey (BBS), a continent-wide bird monitoring program (Sauer et al. 2008), and species distribution information, were used to identify species of high conservation concern at a continental scale (Panjabi et al. 2001).

To assess the status of bird species at regional scales, the Oregon-Washington and California PIF chapters instituted multiple regional monitoring programs. The Klamath Bird Monitoring Network (Network) is an example of such a program (Alexander et al. 2004). The Network was designed to: 1) monitor regional bird population trends for comparison with BBS results; 2) determine the distribution of species of concern in southern Oregon and northern California; and 3) develop habitat relationship models.

The Network facilitated regional assessment using mist-netting and point count data collected with standard protocols (Ralph et al. 1993) employed at different spatial and temporal scales. Regional data from the Network's long-term (>10 year) constant-effort mist-netting stations corroborated BBS data that suggest declines for Swainson's Thrushes (*Catharus ustulatus*), Orange-crowned Warblers (*Vermivora celata*), Black-throated Gray Warblers (*Dendroica nigrescens*), MacGillivray's Warblers (*Oporornis tolmei*), and Purple Finches (*Carpodacus purpureus*) (Klamath Bird Observatory pers. comm.). Point count data refined our knowledge of the distribution and habitat relationships of bird communities in the Klamath-Siskiyou Region. We confirmed that elevation, plant species composition (i.e., habitat type) and vegetation structure are important factors for determining species distribution (Alexander 1999, Seavy 2006).

Results from analyses of population status and habitat requirements of bird species of concern can guide the land management process in the Klamath-Siskiyou Region. They provide a foundation for regional habitat-based conservation plans (Altman 2000a, California Partners in Flight 2002b) and contribute to continental bird conservation planning (Rich et al. 2004). Variables used to describe the distribution of birds (e.g., vegetation structure and volume; Alexander 1999, Seavy 2006) are the same variables used to describe current and desired conditions in the land management planning process.

Effectiveness monitoring results and adaptive management

Land management agencies are required to monitor the effectiveness of their management actions to determine if they are meeting desired ecological conditions (Forest Ecosystem Management Assessment Team 1993). Birds can serve as useful tools when evaluating management actions and designing conservation efforts because they occupy a diversity of ecological niches (Riparian Habitat Joint Venture 2004) and respond to a wide variety of habitat conditions (Hutto 1998). In addition, compared to other taxa, birds are inexpensively detected using standardized sampling protocols (Alexander et al. 2007). Thus, birds serve as "focal species" whose requirements define different spatial attributes, habitat characteristics, and management regimes of healthy ecosystems (Chase and Geupel 2005).

We evaluated the ecological effects of fuel reduction projects in oak woodland and chaparral habitats of the U. S. Bureau of Land Management (BLM) Medford District in the Klamath-Siskiyou Region using point counts, comparing the abundance of PIF focal species in treated and adjacent untreated habitats (Alexander et al. 2007). Our results suggested that small-scale treatments that retained shrub patches benefited edge-associated birds, including regionally declining Purple Finches (Fig. 2). These results corroborated information in the PIF regional bird conservation plan for landbirds in lowlands and valleys (Altman 2000a) regarding the importance of edge habitats for some species. Our data also suggested that the fuel reduction efforts retained shrub patches resulting in no measurable decline in shrub-associated bird species. However, our results did raise a concern about negative impacts of treatments on species that use small snags.

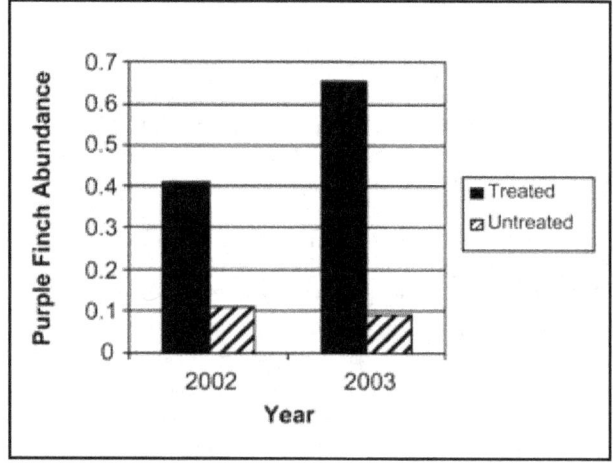

Figure 2. Mean abundance (individuals per station) of Purple Finches detected in hand-pile and burn treatment (51 stations clustered in 9 units) and untreated (49 stations clustered in 7 units) oak woodland and chaparral plots of the Applegate Valley, Oregon, from Alexander et al. (2007).

The BLM Medford District's multi-disciplinary management team incorporated these results into subsequent treatment projects, altering treatment prescriptions to include the retention of small snags (V. Arthur pers. comm.). These revised prescriptions not only addressed the needs of edge and shrub associated species, they also maintained key features for snag associates. Monitoring bird response to land management continues to play a crucial role in the management of oak-shrub-conifer matrix on BLM's Medford District.

Extending the PIF strategy to land managers throughout the Klamath-Siskiyou Region

Federal agencies manage the majority of forested and shrubland landscapes across the west and therefore offer some of the best opportunities to implement bird conservation objectives at large scales. PIF has a long history of partnership with these agencies; however land management decisions do not consistently consider or align with PIF conservation objectives. Increased effectiveness monitoring which uses PIF focal species as indicators of current and desired ecological conditions would result in better informed management decisions with regards to bird conservation.

Encouragingly, in the Klamath-Siskiyou Region, land management agencies are beginning to use the information from the analyses of the Network's data to design oak woodland treatments to be more consistent with PIF habitat-based conservation objectives. Additionally, increased collaborations within the PIF conservation strategy are engaging land managers to evaluate the impacts of other land management projects, including larger-scale fuel reduction treatments in oak woodlands (Seavy et al. 2008) and small-scale fuel reduction treatments in riparian habitats (Klamath Bird Observatory and U.S. Bureau of Land Management 2009). Furthermore, as landscape level fuel reduction programs are being planned regional land managers are consulting with PIF conservation planners to design the spatial distribution and replication of treatments that serve as a frame for well designed effectiveness monitoring studies (Klamath Bird Observatory and U.S. Bureau of Land Management 2009). Thus, the PIF strategy is being more widely incorporated into land management throughout the Klamath-Siskiyou Region.

By integrating the PIF conservation planning strategy within local land management planning processes, the PIF strategy can serve as a catalyst for sustainable land management within the adaptive management framework. Such integration results in three conditions that Williams et al. (2009) suggest are ideal for successful implementation of adaptive management:

(1) Because the use of bird monitoring, as a cost effective tool to monitor the ecological effects of management, is integral to the PIF conservation strategy, it works well within ecosystem management;

(2) PIF conservation planners are engaging management leadership by identifying conservation opportunities within priority land management objectives; and

(3) Broad stakeholder consensus is being built around resulting land management actions that meet both land management and bird conservation objectives.

As a means for supporting land management agency efforts to implement adaptive management the integration of PIF's conservation planning strategy within local land management planning should result in more opportunities to implement bird conservation objectives within land management programs.

Acknowledgments

The Klamath Bird Observatory has worked with the U.S. Forest Service Redwood Sciences Laboratory and many partners to implement the Partners in Flight conservation planning strategy described here through a series of Oregon-Washington and California Partners in Flight projects. These have been supported with funding from U.S. Forest Service, U.S. Bureau of Land Management, and the Joint Fire Sciences Program. Support from Jackson and Klamath counties was provided through the Secure Rural Schools and Community Self-Determination Act of 2000 (Public Law 106-393). Additional support was provided from the National Fish and Wildlife Foundation and the M.J. Murdock Charitable Trust. This success story resulted from long-running collaborative relationships with local Bureau of Land Management and Forest Service partners. Comments from Paul G. Sneed, Rick Medrick, C. John Ralph, Jaime L. Stephens, Michael T. Green, J. Michael Scott, Victoria Sturtevant and three anonymous reviewers greatly improved this manuscript.

Partnering to Conserve Avian Biodiversity in National Parks of the Klamath Region

Daniel Sarr, Sarah McCullough, and Sean Mohren

Abstract

National Park lands are often believed to contribute towards the habitat-based objectives outlined in the Partners in Flight Bird Conservation Plans by protecting large tracks of contiguous land holdings where natural processes predominate. However, a paucity of accurate data to evaluate such assumptions has left the National Park Service's contributions to regional conservation initiatives open to question.

The Klamath Network, a confederation of six National Park Service units in southern Oregon and northern California, launched its Inventory and Monitoring Program in 2000. Since then, the Network has taken four sequential steps to explore patterns of avian biodiversity and to lay the groundwork for long-term landbird monitoring. The steps include: 1) conducting inventories to determine distribution and abundance of relatively common species in the parks; 2) updating the bird species list for each park; 3) designating landbirds as vital signs for the Network; and 4) developing landbird monitoring protocols to guide long-term monitoring.

In 2002, the Klamath Network approached the Klamath Bird Observatory with a request to partner for inventory and monitoring of landbirds. Since then, Klamath Bird Observatory has provided assistance with each of the network steps for the development of its inventory and monitoring program. Through this collaboration, the Klamath Network has been able to meet park management objectives and become an active contributor to Partners in Flight conservation objectives at regional and continental scales.

Background

The National Park Service Inventory and Monitoring Program.—When President Woodrow Wilson signed The Organic Act of 1916, he authorized the formation of a National Park Service (NPS) dedicated to "conserve the scenery and the natural and historic objects and the wild life therein and to provide for the enjoyment of the same in such manner and by such means as will leave them unimpaired for the enjoyment of future generations"

Early park service administrators often assumed that the exclusion of logging, grazing, and mining would ensure, in the words of Horace Albright, second Director of the NPS, that national parks would persist in "everlasting wildness" (Sellars 1997). As early as the 1930s, however; scientific studies showed that this was an invalid presumption (Sellars 1997). Declines in native species (especially predators), introductions of exotic plants and animals, and impacts from roads were noted in the earliest investigations of national parks in California (Sellars 1997). It became apparent that there was a need for quantitative information about the status of park ecosystems, their intrinsic variability, and potential threats. A scarcity of information made it difficult to assess the contributions of the national parks to other regional conservation initiatives such as Partners in Flight (PIF).

To address internal and external demands for scientific information, NPS developed a nationwide Inventory and Monitoring Program (National Park Service 2006a) to yield scientifically sound information on the status and long-term trends of park ecosystems and to determine how well current management practices are sustaining those ecosystems (National Park Service 2008a). As a critical step in the development of the Inventory and Monitoring Program, 270 national park units nationwide were grouped into 32 networks linked by geographic similarities, common natural resources, and resource protection challenges. The network approach was chosen to facilitate staffing, collaboration, information sharing, and economies of scale in natural resource monitoring.

The Klamath Network encompasses six units managed by NPS in northern California and southern Oregon: Crater Lake National Park, Lassen Volcanic National Park, Lava Beds National Monument, Oregon Caves National Monument, Redwood National and State Parks, and Whiskeytown National Recreation Area (National Park Service 2008b). Collectively, the six units comprise nearly 200,000 ha and range considerably in size (196–73,775 ha), relief, and character (Fig. 1). The parks of the Klamath Network span a region of exceptional complexity, where steep climatic, geologic, and topographic gradients and varied disturbance regimes yield biological diversity that is exceeded in few similarly sized areas of the continent

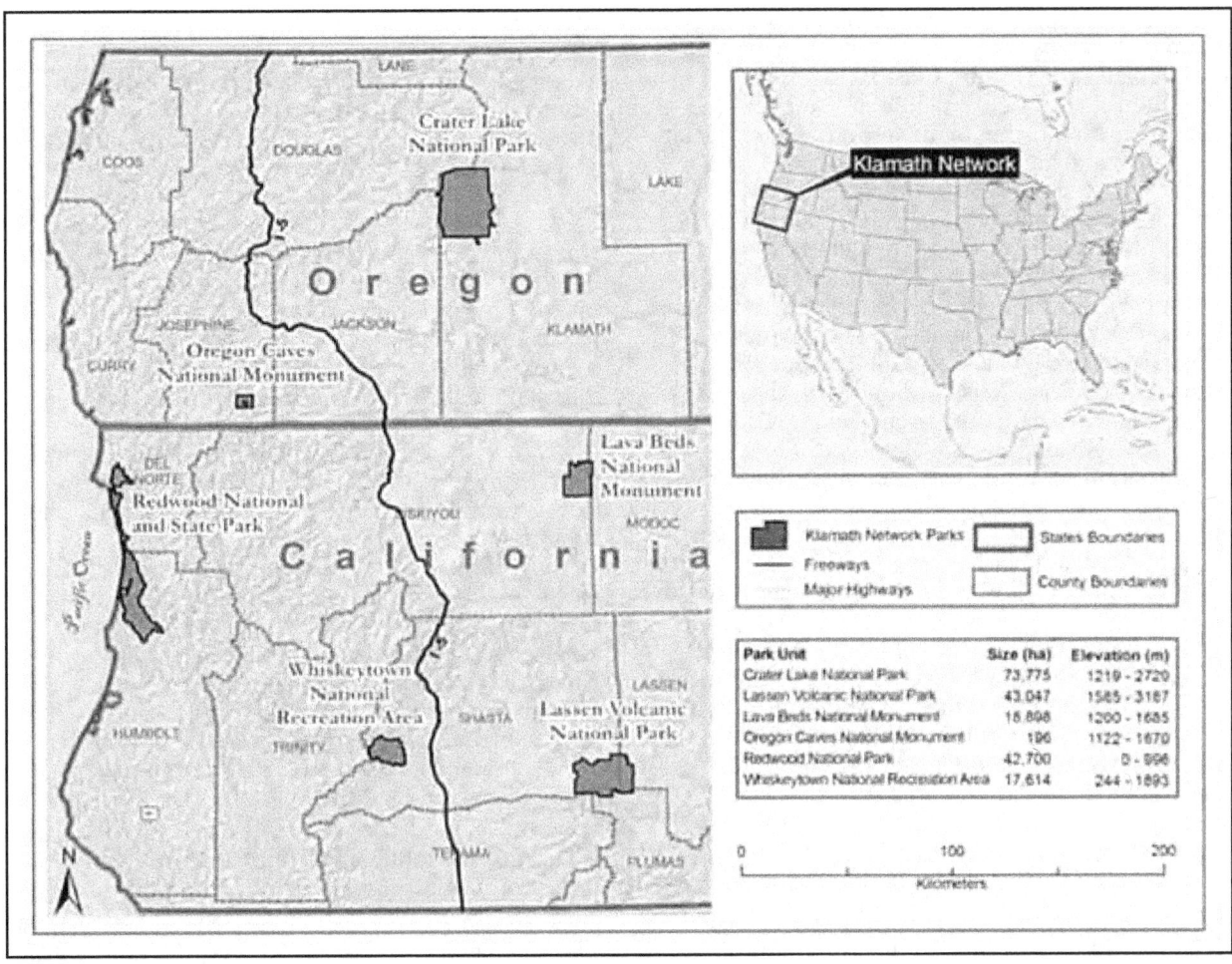

Figure 1. Six National Park Service units in southern Oregon and northern California constitute the Klamath Network.

(DellaSala et al. 1999, Sarr et al. 2004). The parks in the Klamath Network contain a diverse mosaic of climates, landforms, and ecosystems, from moist redwood forests near the coast to xeric sagebrush steppe inland, and from oak woodlands to alpine fell fields (Sarr et al. 2004). This paper describes four steps the Klamath Network, with Klamath Bird Observatory (KBO), has taken to inventory and better understand avian biodiversity in the parks and to lay the groundwork for long-term landbird monitoring.

Inventory needs in the Klamath Network Parks.— The Klamath Network Inventory Program was a five year project funded by NPS from 2000 - 2004 (Ackers et al. 2002, McCullough 2006b). The intent was to develop a current species list of at least 90% accuracy for vascular plants and vertebrates (i.e., birds, mammals, amphibians, reptiles, and fish), and to determine distribution and abundance of taxa of special concern in each park. During initial scoping prior to the launch of the inventory program, the parks of the Klamath Network identified Neotropical migrant birds as a taxon of special concern and primary emphasis for field sampling (Sarr et al. 2007). Neotropical

songbird declines have been reported throughout North America (Ballard et al. 2003) and recent analyses suggest this is also the case in the Klamath-Siskiyou ecoregion (Trail 2004), which is central to the Klamath Network parks. Within this ecoregion, there are a number of potential factors contributing to population declines. Limiting factors include habitat loss and alteration, land uses that compromise the integrity of natural systems such as overgrazing, development, and suppression of natural processes (e.g., fire, flooding), nest parasitism by Brown-headed Cowbirds (*Molothrus ater*), competition from invading species (e.g. Barred Owls (*Strix varia*) supplanting Northern Spotted Owls (*Strix occidentalis caurina*)), and predation by both native and non-native predators (Sarr et al. 2007). For these reasons, the parks in the Klamath Network desired a better understanding of the current status of landbirds within their boundaries and at a regional scale. In addition, the Network desired baseline landbird data to support potential monitoring in the future.

Partnering with Klamath Bird Observatory.— When confronted with the need to inventory landbirds in the parks within the Klamath Network, partnering with KBO was a logical choice. KBO has been operating a network of bird monitoring stations throughout the Klamath-Siskiyou region of California and Oregon since 1993. More importantly, their dedication to providing science-based bird monitoring to further bird conservation and help make land management decisions is a central interest to NPS, as well as to other Federal agencies. Both the NPS and KBO are involved in PIF, a conservation initiative dedicated to increasing the cooperative efforts of public and private organizations involved in bird conservation. The lands within the Klamath Network parks are extraordinarily diverse, falling under six regional PIF Bird Conservation Plans, the Oak Woodland, Riparian, Coniferous Forest, Coastal Scrub, Sagebrush, and the East-slope Cascades conservation plans and two biomes (Pacific and Intermountain West) listed in the PIF North American Landbird Conservation Plan (Altman 1999, 2000c; California Partners in Flight 2002a, 2002b; Riparian Habitat Joint Venture 2004; Rich et al. 2005). Accurate information about the distribution and abundance of landbirds in the Klamath Network parks was considered essential to helping the parks meet their inventory goals while contributing to PIF efforts to conserve and improve our understanding and conservation of focal bird species.

Implementing the landbird inventory.—During a two year field effort conducted in 2002 – 2003, KBO scientists established study areas in riparian and adjacent upland habitats and used multiple avian survey methods that varied by park in order to maximize the inventory data in each park. Methods were determined based on park size, variability in park habitat, and to align with monitoring methods used in the past. The objective of the inventory was to obtain baseline data on the distribution and abundance of target species during both the breeding and migration seasons. KBO also conducted constant-effort mist netting at Oregon Caves National Monument, summarized datasets from previous bird monitoring efforts in three parks, and compared the results from the 2002 and 2003 field seasons to existing species lists for each park.

During the two year inventory, a total of 234 new landbird inventory stations were established in Crater Lake National Park and Whiskeytown National Recreational Area. At Lava Beds National Monument, 36 fall migration bird area search inventory stations were established (overlapping with existing breeding season stations) to create a baseline for fall migration data. For each station that was established, habitat composition and structure data were collected, and GPS data were recorded. Standardized methodologies were used to facilitate replication by future inventory or monitoring efforts. In addition, KBO added to available baseline data by summarizing previous point count efforts in Lassen Volcanic, Crater Lake, and Redwood national parks.

At Oregon Caves National Monument, a constant-effort mist netting station with 10 nets added to existing baseline breeding season and migration season data. It was anticipated that multiyear data would assist potential monitoring, so mist netting was funded in each year since 2003, with a five year summary report completed in 2007 (Frey et al. 2007).

Documenting Avian Biodiversity in the Klamath Network Parks.—The inventories conducted by KBO recorded several new species for the parks and confirmed many species considered hypothetical (Sarr et al. 2004). In addition to its role in implementing field inventories, KBO assisted the Network in a certification process whereby species lists were reviewed for accuracy. Once field inventories and certification processes were complete, the parks had current information about the presence, distribution, and abundance of many of the more common landbird species in the parks (National Park Service 2009). These data, together with park-specific historical data and knowledge, provided an excellent inventory for the Klamath Network that has been of direct relevance to management and subsequent monitoring development efforts. In addition, standardized survey methods were field tested on-the-ground in parks for potential use in long-term monitoring.

Developing a landbird monitoring program

Upon completion of the five year inventory programs, each of the 32 networks in the NPS Inventory and Monitoring Program was provided with base funding to support the development of a long-term Vital Signs Monitoring Program. Development of a monitoring program tasked each Inventory and Monitoring network with convening the parks, regional universities, and other conservation science organizations to identify "vital signs" to monitor as a way to gauge the health of the park ecosystems. Ongoing examples of such vital signs monitoring include tracking air and water quality, climate, and population dynamics of small mammals or waterfowl, and studying historical photographic records.

During the initial scoping meetings, the Klamath Network park representatives recognized landbirds as a key resource that could provide valuable information about the park's ecosystems through long-term monitoring. In addition, they recognized that landbird conservation requires a perspective that extends to the regional and continental scale, well beyond park boundaries.

The Vital Signs Process

The Klamath Network vital signs selection process began in 2004. The process involved 130 experts representing a broad array of scientific disciplines and required them to rank candidate vital signs (biological communities or ecological components of the parks) based on ecological and management significance (National Park Service 2006b). The final selection of vital signs was accomplished at a

Table 1. Top ten vital signs (biological communities or ecological components of the parks) of the Klamath Network based on ecological and management significance (National Park Service 2006).

Ranking	Vital Signs
1	Non-native species
2	Keystone and sensitive plants and animals
3	Terrestrial vegetation
4	Bird communities
5	Intertidal communities
6	Freshwater aquatic communities
7	Cave collapse / entrance communities
8	Water quality (aquatic, marine and subterranean)
9	Land cover, use, pattern
10	Environmental conditions in caves

workshop in Redding, California on 27-28 April 2005, where NPS staff reviewed and approved the final list: bird communities ranked fourth in importance to the parks, out of over 100 vital signs (Table 1). Landbird communities were selected as a focal community important to maintaining and measuring ecological integrity in terrestrial ecosystems. Bird communities are species-rich, easy to monitor compared to other kinds of communities, present in most park habitats, and can serve as indicators of environmental change (Temple and Wiens 1989). Long-term monitoring of species composition, population trends, and distributions of landbird communities will provide valuable information on population responses to natural and anthropogenic influences within and outside of park boundaries.

Developing a Landbird Monitoring Protocol.— In 2007, KBO began assisting the Network with the development of a landbird monitoring protocol for the parks. Under the protocol process, KBO and the Network have developed spatial and temporal sampling designs for each park, standard data analysis and reporting practices, and a comprehensive data management system that contributes information for local, regional, national, and continental needs (Stephens et al. 2009). Implementation of the protocol began in the spring of 2008.

Collaborative conservation in the Klamath Region

Since 1993, KBO and the U.S. Forest Service's Redwood Sciences Laboratory have been coordinating bird monitoring efforts in the Klamath-Siskiyou region. Known as the Klamath Demographic Monitoring Network, this effort has yielded a substantial regional dataset (Alexander et al. 2004). The NPS vital signs bird monitoring program, although designed to answer park-specific questions, will contribute to monitoring bird distribution and population trend information being gathered by KBO at the regional scale. The nesting of the NPS vital signs monitoring program within the larger Klamath Demographic Monitoring Network provides an opportunity to explore questions about the effects of habitat management and environmental conditions on landbird populations across a large landscape.

Moreover, the NPS Vital Signs Monitoring Program will complement the PIF goals both materially and conceptually; their approaches are complementary. The overall goal of PIF bird conservation planning is to ensure long-term conservation of native landbirds (Rich et al. 2004). The vital signs process is intended to provide a broad view of the integrity of park ecosystems. Vital signs monitoring of landbirds in the Klamath Network parks will work toward both these broad and interdependent goals. Quantitative information about landbird distribution and abundance, managed in high quality databases developed in partnership with KBO, will allow the NPS to meet its local management needs and to make substantial contributions to regional and continental bird conservation.

Use of Bird Conservation Plans for Development of Management Plans for National Wildlife Refuges in Washington, Oregon, and California

Michael T. Green, Kevin Kilbride, and Fred Paveglio

Abstract

The National Wildlife Refuge System is in the midst of developing and revising resource planning documents, including Comprehensive Conservation Plans to guide long-term management, Habitat Management Plans which add detail to the Comprehensive Conservation Plans, and Environmental Assessments for specific activities. Each of these planning documents offers opportunities for setting specific biological targets for management. Partners in Flight and shorebird and waterbird initiatives have developed conservation plans that provide land managers with information to improve habitat conditions for birds. Increasingly, refuge staff and planners with the U.S. Fish and Wildlife Service in California, Oregon, and Washington are using objectives from the bird conservation plans to develop detailed refuge objectives in resource planning documents. Using focal species from bird conservation plans to guide the development of habitat objectives will enable land managers to recreate functioning ecosystems in priority habitats. In addition, monitoring the habitat and landbird responses to the conservation recommendations provides feedback for assessing their effectiveness. We present examples from four National Wildlife Refuges that incorporated Partners in Flight plans into refuge planning documents: Little Pend Oreille, Klamath Marsh, Sacramento River, and San Joaquin River.

Introduction

Under the jurisdiction of the U.S. Fish and Wildlife Service, all National Wildlife Refuges (refuges) are developing, or have recently developed, Comprehensive Conservation Plans (CCPs) to guide long-term management in accordance with the National Wildlife Refuge System Improvement Act (1997). In addition, refuges are updating Habitat Management Plans (HMPs). CCPs typically have a 15-year planning horizon and updated HMPs add detail to management prescriptions that are presented as strategies within CCPs. Furthermore, the National Environmental Policy Act (1970) requires Environmental Assessments (EAs) for some refuge activities. Each of these resource planning documents offers opportunities for setting specific biological targets for management. At the same time, Partners in Flight (PIF) and initiatives to conserve waterbirds and shorebirds have developed conservation plans that strive to provide land managers with information that will translate into improved habitat management for birds. Increasingly, refuge staff and planners in California, Oregon, and Washington are using bird conservation plans from PIF and the other bird initiatives to develop detailed refuge objectives in CCPs, HMPs, and EAs. While many refuges were established for the purposes of conserving species other than birds (e.g., Hart Mountain National Antelope Refuge), many others have purposes related directly to migratory birds through the Migratory Bird Conservation Act (1929). In addition, each refuge has at least a secondary responsibility to consider the needs of birds on their lands through the trust responsibility endowed upon the U.S. Fish and Wildlife Service for the protection, conservation, and management of migratory birds through the Migratory Bird Treaty Act (1918). Thus, management for migratory birds is a prominent feature of many refuge planning documents.

The PIF plans for California, Oregon, and Washington provide detailed strategies to meet life history requirements for high-priority (e.g. focal) landbirds in priority habitats, habitats which have generally been substantially altered relative to pre-European settlement. The habitat requirements of focal species represent spatial attributes, habitat conditions, and management regimes characteristic of healthy ecosystems (Riparian Habitat Joint Venture 2004). Thus, by using focal species to guide the development of habitat objectives on refuges, land managers can recreate functioning ecosystems in these priority habitats. Monitoring the habitat response and responses of bird populations to the PIF conservation recommendations provides invaluable feedback for assessing their effectiveness.

The following are examples from refuges in Washington, Oregon, and California that have used PIF bird conservation plans for the development of recent refuge planning documents.

Little Pend Oreille National Wildlife Refuge

Established in 1939 as a "refuge and breeding ground for migratory birds and other wildlife," (U.S. Fish and Wildlife Service 2000) Little Pend Oreille National Wildlife Refuge comprises 16,268 ha of cold, moist, and dry forests along with alluvial riparian and some meadow habitat. It lies 100 km north of Spokane, Washington, and is surrounded by U.S. Forest Service lands, including the Colville National Forest.

The CCP for this refuge was developed in 2000 (U.S. Fish and Wildlife Service 2000), and describes long-term habitat management and restoration goals, objectives, and strategies for its forested, riparian, and wetland habitats. The 2005 HMP further refines the CCP objectives (U.S. Fish and Wildlife Service 2005a) and draws heavily from the Oregon-Washington PIF landbird plan for the northern Rocky Mountain region (Altman 2000b). The HMP used all of the focal landbird species and their habitat objectives in this bird conservation plan except for Upland Sandpipers (*Bartramia longicauda*) and Vesper Sparrows (*Pooecetes gramineus*), which lack appropriate habitat on the refuge.

Habitat objectives in the HMP are derived from habitat requirements for several focal species in the PIF plan, but the most striking use of the PIF plan for the HMP is the refuge's long-term habitat objective for ponderosa pine (*Pinus ponderosa*). Ponderosa pine dominated, late-seral dry forest is a habitat type considerably reduced in the Northwest due to logging and fire suppression (O'Neil et al. 2001). White-headed Woodpeckers (*Picoides albolarvatus*) are the focal species representing healthy ponderosa pine forests in late-seral condition in the PIF plan. It has also shown local population declines, and is a conservation priority in this region (Rich et al. 2004, U.S. Fish and Wildlife Service 2008). The prescription for the habitat attributes in the HMP, as described for White-headed Woodpeckers in the PIF plan (Altman 2000b), are to provide 1821 ha in patches larger than 142 ha through periodic thinning and burning of mid-seral stage forest (Fig. 1), and that these late-seral dry forest stands have:

"10 or more trees per acre larger than 53 cm dbh, with at least two of those exceeding 79 cm dbh; 10–40% tree canopy cover; and more than 1.4 snags per acre that are greater than 20 cm dbh."

By achieving this habitat objective, refuge lands would provide protected habitat needed by 5 to 12 pairs of White-headed Woodpeckers where there are none now (calculated from home range estimates; Garrett et al. 1996). This objective is striking not only because of its required 100–200 year time frame, but also for its degree of specificity. The long time frame is appropriate for developing stands of old-growth ponderosa pine, but unusually far-sighted for a refuge and well beyond the 15-year scope of most CCPs.

Point counts were conducted by refuge staff from 2000 – 2002, and will continue periodically as restoration continues. A long-term monitoring strategy will allow for the evaluation of the effectiveness of the habitat restorations, and of the habitat recommendations in the bird conservation plan. If White-headed Woodpeckers do not respond as expected, habitat restorations will be examined, simultaneously with the habitat prescriptions suggested for this species in the bird conservation plan.

Klamath Marsh National Wildlife Refuge

The Klamath Marsh National Wildlife Refuge is one of six refuges in the Klamath Basin National Wildlife Refuge Complex located in southern Oregon and northern California. The Klamath Marsh refuge lies about 50 km north of Klamath Falls, Oregon. The refuge was established in 1958 to provide migration and production habitat for migratory birds, particularly waterfowl and Sandhill Cranes (*Grus canadensis*). The 16,502 ha refuge is 90% permanent and seasonal marsh, with a 1376 ha fringe of forest characterized by lodgepole pine (*Pinus contorta*), ponderosa pine, and relict quaking aspen (*Populus tremuloides*). Winema National Forest and private lands border the refuge, and nearby farms and ranches grow hay and livestock.

A fuels reduction EA (U.S. Fish and Wildlife Service 2003) was developed to protect refuge structures and neighboring residences from wildfires, and to restore and maintain the condition of wildlife habitats including old-growth ponderosa pine and lodgepole pine, aspen stands, and seasonally-wet meadows. As elsewhere in the West (Covington and Moore 1994, Fleischner 1994), the condition of pine forests and aspen woodlands on the refuge have declined due largely to fire suppression and grazing pressure. Several bird species would benefit from proper aspen management, e.g., removing heavy grazing pressure (Earnst et al. 2005, Heltzel and Earnst 2006). Decadent aspen groves also regenerate rapidly when challenged with controlled burns and cutting of competing species of conifer (Jones and DeByle 1985). Bird species likely to benefit from management for aspen include Western Screech-Owls (*Otus kennicottii*), Northern Pygmy Owls (*Glaucidium gnoma*), Williamson's Sapsuckers (*Sphyrapicus thyroideus*), Red-naped Sapsuckers (*Sphyrapicus nuchalis*), Northern Flickers (*Colaptes auratus*), Tree Swallows (*Tachycineta bicolor*), House Wrens (*Troglodytes aedon*), and Mountain Bluebirds (*Sialia currucoides*) (Altman 2000c). Appendix 1 of the EA describes in detail the desired conditions for each of those habitats, their associated focal bird species, and treatment options (thinning and burning) to achieve those conditions. In aspen, for example, the desired future condition in the EA is "large aspen trees and snags with regeneration" to benefit Red-naped Sapsuckers.

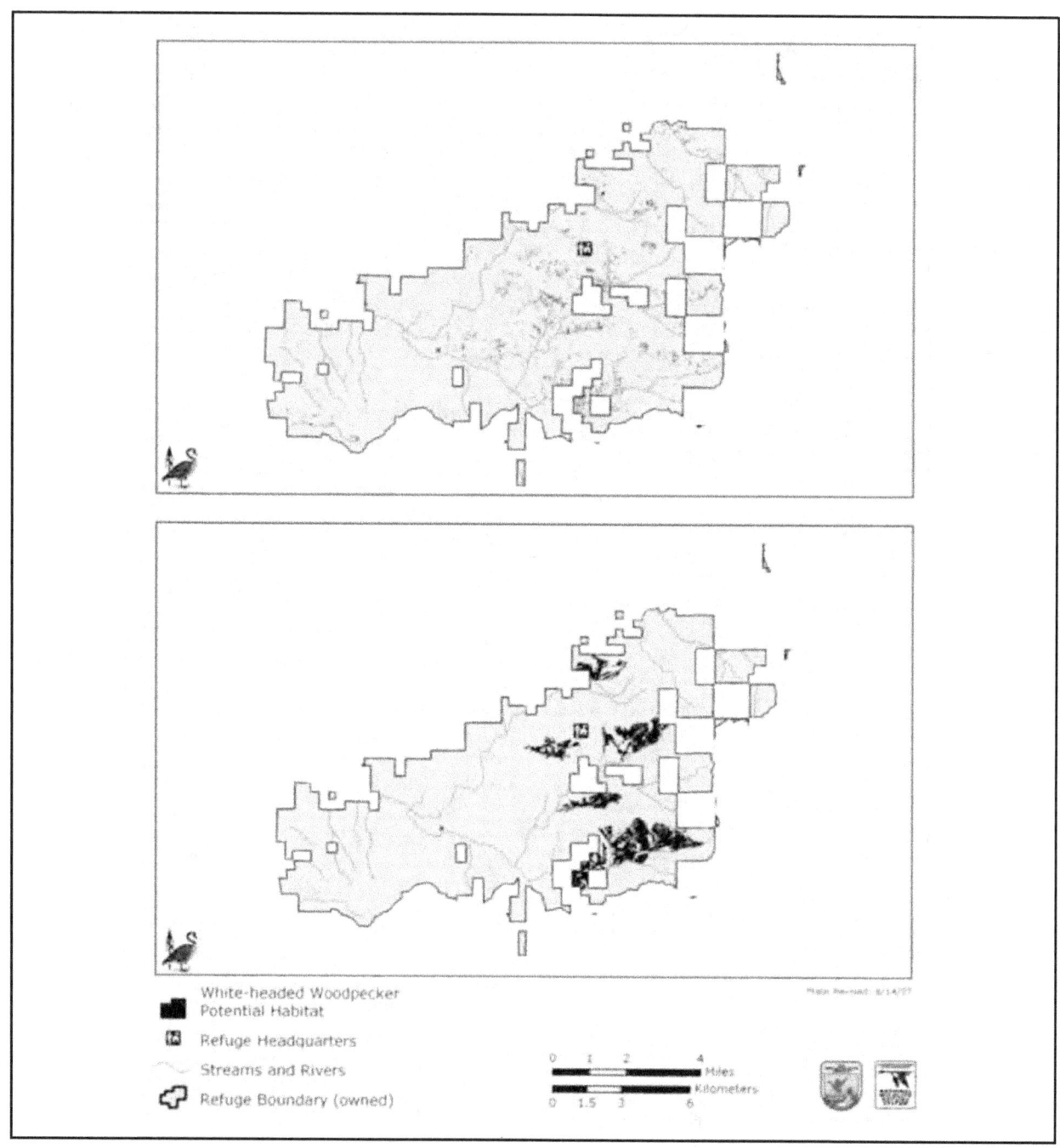

Figure 1. On Little Pend Oreille National Wildlife Refuge, the extent of old growth ponderosa pine and potential habitat of White-headed Woodpeckers (>80 ha contiguous forest) now (above) and in 100-200 years.

The habitat objective includes the following habitat attributes (Altman 2000c):

"... to maintain or provide some areas with natural (e.g., fire) or mechanical disturbance regimes to ensure proper successional development... > 10% cover of sapling aspen in the understory to provide adequate representation of younger seral stages for replacement; > 4 trees and > 1.5 snags/ac > 12 m in height and 25 cm dbh; mean canopy cover 40-80% —either clumped with patches and openings or relatively evenly distributed."

Klamath Bird Observatory conducted baseline bird monitoring in future aspen restoration sites from 2003 – 2005 including 140 point count stations during the spring and 70 area search plots during the fall (Stephens and Alexander 2006). Monitoring will continue periodically after habitat management strategies commence to evaluate the efficacy of the treatments in achieving the desired habitat conditions and to assess the recommendations in the bird conservation plan for creating habitat for Red-breasted Sapsuckers and other species associated with aspen.

Sacramento River and San Joaquin River National Wildlife Refuges

These two refuges conserve riverine and floodplain habitats along the Sacramento and San Joaquin rivers in California's Central Valley. Sacramento River National Wildlife Refuge currently manages approximately 4654 ha in 26 units along the Sacramento River from Red Bluff south to Princeton, California, and could expand to 7284 ha based upon the approved boundary. The San Joaquin River National Wildlife Refuge lies in the historic floodplain of the confluence of the San Joaquin, Stanislaus, and Tuolumne rivers and comprises 2428 ha west of Modesto, California in Merced County; the approved boundary includes 5180 ha. Both refuges are important foci for riparian restoration in California, and are identified as conservation portfolio sites in the Riparian Bird Conservation Plan (Riparian Habitat Joint Venture 2004).

The staff of the Sacramento River National Wildlife Refuge drew upon nearly 15 years of riparian restoration experience for development of the CCP (U.S. Fish and Wildlife Service 2005b). Since 1993, the refuge has restored approximately 1335 ha (mostly in recently acquired orchards) of riparian vegetation within the historic Sacramento River floodplain. The Riparian Bird Habitat Conservation Plan (Riparian Habitat Joint Venture 2004) provided significant guidance on appropriate restoration techniques to address the habitat needs of riparian focal species. PRBO Conservation Science (PRBO) is monitoring the bird response to the restoration to direct future management and restoration efforts in an adaptive management framework. Approximately 1214 additional hectares are planned for restoration efforts through 2015 with management strategies to be derived directly from the Riparian Bird Conservation Plan (Riparian Habitat Joint Venture 2004, U.S. Fish and Wildlife Service 2005b, Gardali et al. 2006).

In completing the CCP for the San Joaquin River National Wildlife Refuge, the staff was able to include the results of riparian restoration efforts guided by the Riparian Bird Conservation Plan (Riparian Habitat Joint Venture 2004) and monitoring provided by PRBO (U.S. Fish and Wildlife Service 2007). Riparian restoration at this refuge resulted in the first recorded nesting of endangered Least Bell's Vireos *(Vireo bellii pusillus)* in the Central Valley in over 60 years (U.S. Fish and Wildlife Service 2005c). The restoration incorporated native riparian vegetation such as mugwort *(Artemisia douglasiana)*, California wild rose *(Rosa californica)*, arroyo willow *(Salix lasiolepis)*, and valley oak *(Quercus lobata)*; plant species known to benefit riparian-associated birds. The restoration design also integrated the Riparian Bird Conservation Plan recommendation to promote a dense, shrubby understory, an important component in the breeding habitat of Least Bell's Vireos (Kreitinger and Wood 2005). The documentation of Least Bell's Vireos breeding at the San Joaquin River National Wildlife Refuge underscores the role that proper habitat restoration and management can play in conserving biodiversity.

Conclusion

The use of PIF plans to facilitate the development of long-term management plans on refuges in Oregon, Washington, and California is a PIF success story. The mission of the Fish and Wildlife Service is "Working with others to conserve, protect, and enhance fish, wildlife, and plants and their habitats for the continuing benefit of the American people…" (U.S. Fish and Wildlife Service 1999) and the Service has primary conservation and management responsibilities for the nation's migratory birds. Thus, the adoption of PIF management recommendations into their own planning documents is a natural union. However, PIF bird conservation plans, and plans from waterbird and shorebird initiatives, provide solutions not just for National Wildlife Refuge managers, but for all land managers tasked with meeting agency requirements for wildlife management and conserving focal species or birds of high conservation priority.

The responses of birds to management in quick-growing riparian habitats can be measured within a few years; Sacramento and San Joaquin river refuges are good examples. Projects designed to create old-growth conditions in younger forests, such as at Little Pend Oreille National Wildlife Refuge, will take much longer to measure. Regardless, it is important to incorporate a pre- and post-treatment effectiveness monitoring into any major project, at the very least to measure changes in habitat and bird abundance. The iterative loop linking planning to management and monitoring, fundamental to good land management and bird conservation, will only be powerful with all three components

Risk Analysis of Birds Associated with Older Forests of the Pacific Northwest

Martin G. Raphael

Abstract

A team of scientists and managers used research data on the relative abundance of birds in relation to structural stage and forest attributes to list species associated with older forest and to evaluate the likelihood of long-term persistence of those species under a range of forest management alternatives. This knowledge helped craft the final design of the Northwest Forest Plan. Research and monitoring have been essential to the adaptive management process, which is an inherent component of the forest plan. Although monitoring of the two federally listed species Marbled Murrelets (*Brachyramphus marmoratus*) and Northern Spotted Owls (*Strix occidentalis caurina*) is ongoing, there remains a need to evaluate whether the plan has been successful in meeting the needs of other forest birds.

Introduction

During the years leading to the implementation of the Northwest Forest Plan in 1994, timber cutting and other operations on federally managed lands had largely been brought to a halt by federal court orders. At issue was concern for the conservation of biological diversity, especially for those species that might be closely associated with older forests. In response, President Clinton formed the Forest Ecosystem Management Assessment Team (FEMAT), and gave the team an objective to craft land management options (including harvesting) that would maintain or enhance biological diversity, particularly that of late-successional and old-growth ecosystems. To meet this objective, the team was chartered to develop options that would maintain and/or restore habitat conditions to support viable populations, well-distributed across their current ranges, of species known (or reasonably expected) to be associated with old-growth forest conditions (Forest Ecosystem Management Assessment Team 1993). This project covered federal lands within the range of Northern Spotted Owls (*Strix occidentalis caurina*), a total area of about 23 million ha, of which 10 million ha is federal land mostly west of the Cascade crest in Washington, Oregon, and California. The challenges the team faced were to first compile a list of species that were associated with older forest within the project area, and then to conduct an assessment of risk to population viability for each species under each of the proposed options.

The compilation of a list of birds potentially associated with older forest began with the naming of a terrestrial science team as part of the overall FEMAT. This team comprised biologists from the Forest Service, Bureau of Land Management, National Park Service, Fish and Wildlife Service, National Marine Fisheries Service, Environmental Protection Agency, and various universities.

The terrestrial team compiled a list of 119 species of birds that were thought to be associated with forests in the plan area. The team then applied a set of criteria to judge whether each species was closely associated with older forest (Thomas et al. 1993, Forest Ecosystem Management Assessment Team 1993). These criteria included:

(1) The species was statistically more abundant in older forest than in younger forest in any part of its range.

(2) The species reached highest abundance in older forest (but not necessarily statistically so) and required habitat components that are contributed by older forest.

(3) The species was associated with older forest and was on a federal or state threatened, endangered, or sensitive species list.

(3) Strength of association with older forest was unknown, but the species was listed as threatened or endangered and the team had reason to suspect the species was associated with older forest.

Of the original list of 119 species, 38 met one or more of these criteria and were thereby classified as closely associated with older forest (Thomas et al. 1993).

Management Goals

The FEMAT developed a set of 10 land management options that varied in the size and distribution of blocks of land reserved from timber harvest (Fig. 1) as well as specifications for logging and other silvicultural procedures. The terrestrial science team was tasked with assessing the likelihood that

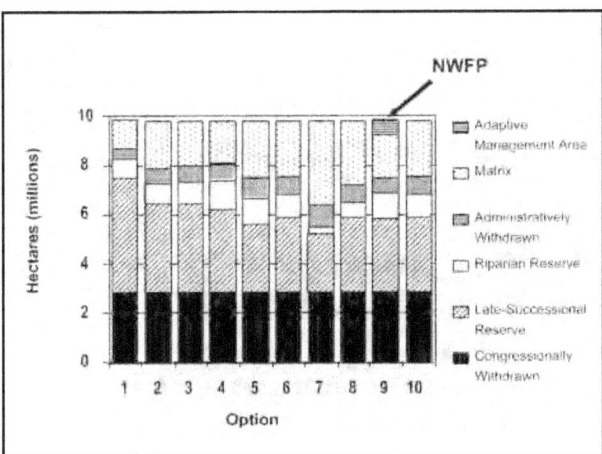

Figure 1. Comparison of amounts of federal land in various allocations in each of 10 land management options considered by Forest Ecosystem Management Assessment Team (1993). Lands designated as matrix and adaptive management areas are generally available for timber harvest, whereas all other allocations are generally reserved from harvest.

habitat conditions would support stable and well-distributed populations of each species of bird under each of the land management options. Detailed assessments were completed for seven of the ten options; the remaining three options (options 2, 6, 10) were relatively minor variations of other options and did not require full assessments. These viability assessments, conducted for birds as well as for other vertebrates and invertebrates, were used to help rank the relative contributions of the seven options to overall biodiversity (Fig. 2). Results of this assessment had a key influence on the final

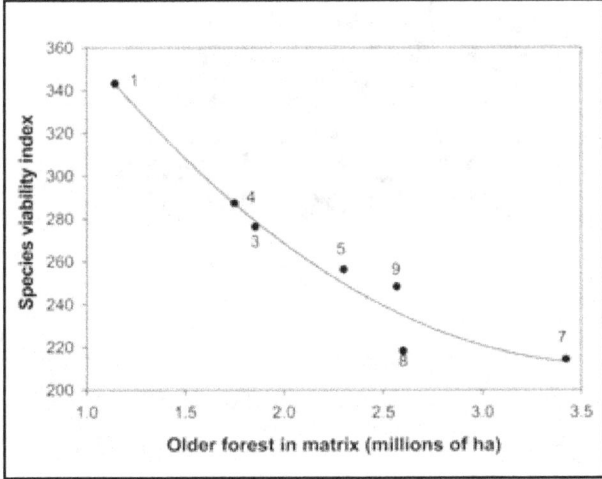

Figure 2. Relationship between species viability (number of species of all taxa with > 60% likelihood of habitat of sufficient quality to support stable and well-distributed populations over 100 years) and amount of land allocated outside of reserves (matrix, see Fig. 1) for 7 of the 10 land management options considered in Forest Ecosystem Management Assessment Team (1993).

decision by the Secretaries of the Departments of Interior and Agriculture to adopt Option 9, which ultimately was implemented as the Northwest Forest Plan (U.S. Department of Agriculture and U.S. Department of the Interior 1994a).

Monitoring Regime

Application of the four criteria cited above required that FEMAT gather information on relative abundance of forest birds in relation to structural stage and on specific habitat elements used by each species. Fortunately, several large scale habitat relationships summaries and sampling programs had been completed recently (Thomas 1979, Marcot 1984, Brown 1985, Raphael et al. 1988, Ralph et al. 1991, Ruggiero et al. 1991), which FEMAT relied upon to make the determinations of species' association with older forest.

The field studies (Marcot 1984, Raphael et al. 1988, Ralph et al. 1991, Ruggiero et al. 1991) employed approximately comparable sampling strategies. In each study, a large number of plots were replicated within a range of early to late seral stages, including both managed and unmanaged stands. Within each plot, a set of sample stations was established and the investigators conducted variable-radius point counts during the breeding season to estimate relative density of each bird species by seral stage. Studies were carried out over 3-5 years. The combination of studies incorporated locations throughout the Northwest Forest Plan area.

Separate assessments were conducted for the two listed species, Marbled Murrelets (*Brachyramphus marmoratus*) and Northern Spotted Owls. For these assessments, the species experts relied on published and unpublished studies, including ongoing monitoring results, to make their determinations (Forest Ecosystem Management Assessment Team 1993).

Response to Management

The FEMAT organized a panel of ornithologists to perform a subjective evaluation of the likelihood that each land management option would provide habitat conditions to support stable and well-distributed populations over the life of the plan (the next 100 years). Panelists relied on information about each option (e.g., extent of reserve system, special management provisions, projected habitat trends), as provided by the FEMAT. They also relied on data from the bird counts cited above. After reviewing available materials and publications, the panelists discussed each species in turn, and arrived at a consensus score for each option, distributing 100 "points" among four possible outcomes:

(A) The species is stable and well-distributed on federal lands;

(B) The species is stable but with significant gaps in distribution with some limitation on population dispersal;

(C) The species is restricted to smaller, isolated refugia with significant limitations on population interactions among refugia;

(D) The species is extirpated from federal lands.

Outcomes for Marbled Murrelets (Fig. 3A) and Northern Spotted Owls (Fig. 3B) were poorest for options 7 and 8. Option 1, in which virtually all older forest was protected from logging, had the highest likelihood of outcome A for Marbled Murrelets and the second highest likelihood for Northern Spotted Owls. Option 9, which formed the basis of the Northwest Forest Plan, had an intermediate likelihood of outcome A for both species. Each of the options was projected to support stable and well-distributed populations (outcome A) of a majority of the other (not listed as either threatened or endangered) bird species (Fig. 3C). None of these birds was projected to have any likelihood of outcomes C or D. Options 7 and 8, which had the lowest amount of land in reserves, had four and nine species, respectively, with likelihoods of 20% or greater in outcome B. Option 9, the Northwest Forest Plan, had only one species, Black-backed Woodpeckers (*Picoides arcticus*), with 20% or greater likelihood of outcome B.

Implementation of results

Option 9 was selected as the preferred alternative in the Environmental Impact Statement that followed the FEMAT plan (U.S. Department of Agriculture and U.S. Department of the Interior 1994a, 1994b). Specific provisions to augment or meet habitat requirements of forest birds were added to the original design of option 9 during the transition from the FEMAT to the Record of Decision. For Marbled Murrelets and Northern Spotted Owls a rigorous monitoring program was implemented (Lint et al. 1999, Madsen et al. 1999) and both habitat and population monitoring continues to this day (Lint 2005, Haynes et al. 2006, Huff et al. 2006, Miller et al. 2006, Noon and Blakesley 2006, Raphael 2006a, Falxa et al. 2009). Results of this monitoring have been essential to managers in their evaluation of the success of the forest plan in meeting its original objectives for species and habitat conservation. For Marbled Murrelets, monitoring has indicated that populations over the bird's range in Washington, Oregon, and California have declined from 2000 to 2008 (Fig. 4). Monitoring shows that Northern Spotted Owl populations have declined from 1985 to 2003 but that the rates vary across the range (Fig. 5). Northern Spotted Owl populations are declining at the greatest rate in the northern part of the range, at intermediate rates in the middle of the range, and may be stable in the southern range (Fig. 5). For both Marbled Murrelets and Northern Spotted Owls the forest plan has been successful in conserving most of the higher-quality nesting habitat within its reserve system on federal lands. For both species, however, conditions outside

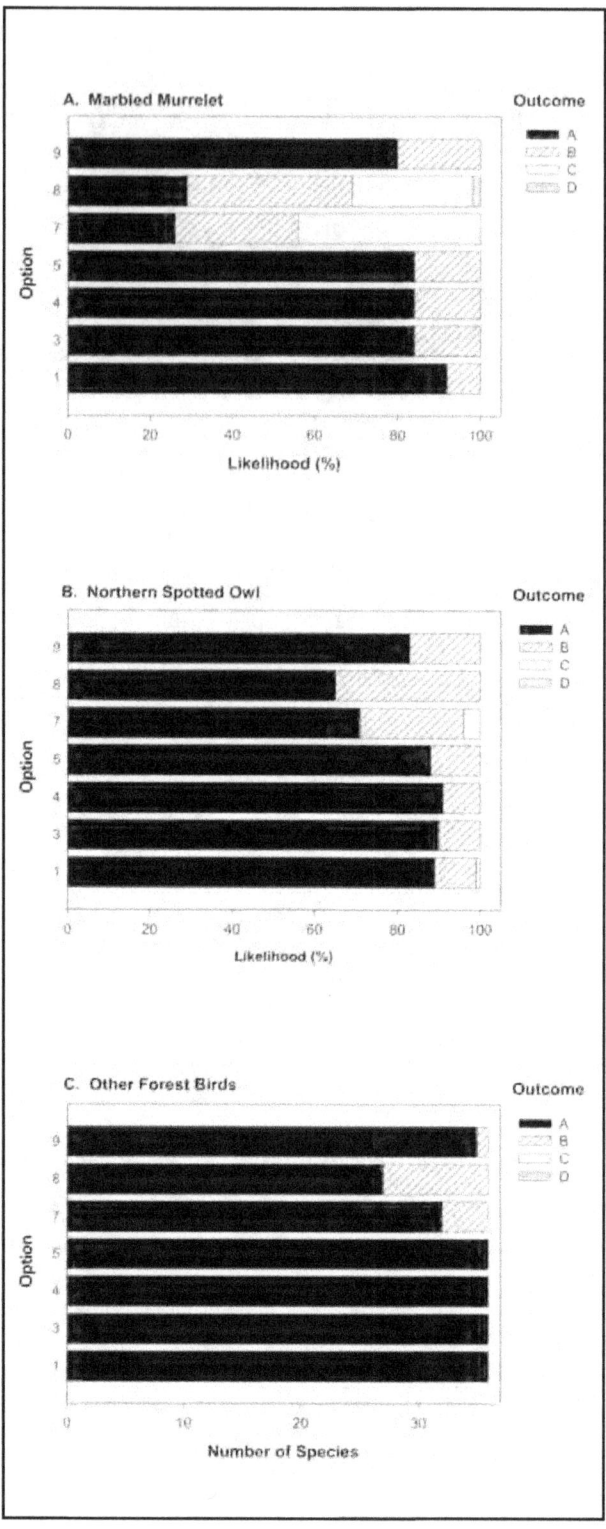

Figure 3. Predicted outcomes of each management option for distribution and persistence of populations over 100 years. 3A: Marbled Murrelets; 3B: Northern Spotted Owls; 3C: the 38 other forest birds (Forest Ecosystem Management Assessment Team 1993). Likelihood, as indicated on the x-axis, is the mean likelihood score calculated from the data recorded by individual panelists.

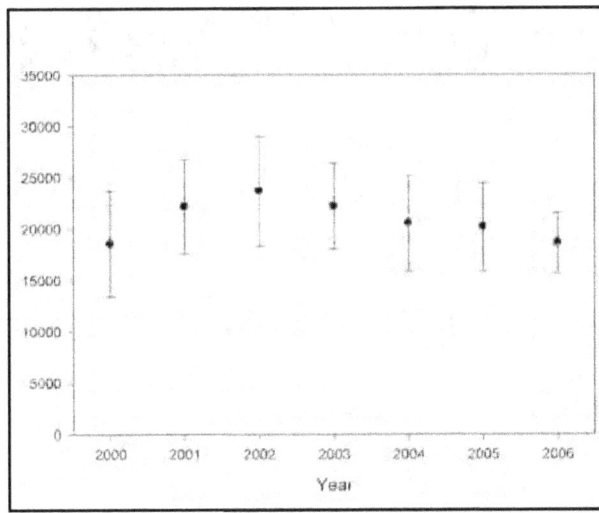

Figure 4. Population estimates and 95% confidence intervals from rangewide at-sea Marbled Murrelet surveys (Falxa et al. 2009).

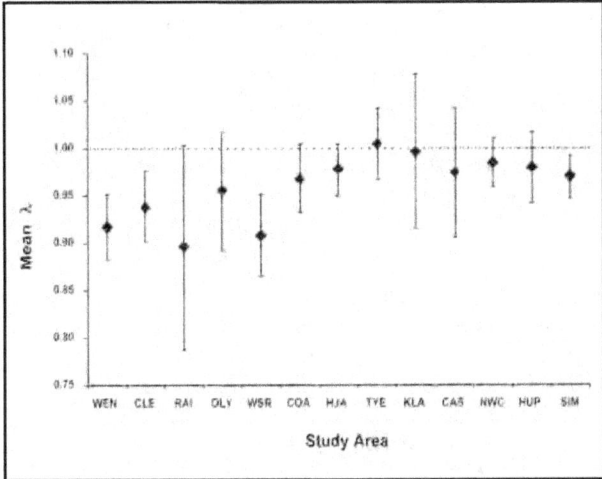

Figure 5. Estimates of mean lambda (, finite rate of population change, with 95% confidence intervals) for Northern Spotted Owls on 13 study areas in Washington (WEN, CLE, RAI, OLY), Oregon (WSR, COA, HJA, TYE, KLA, CAS), and California (NWC, HUP, SIM). The dashed line indicates the level for a stable population; values below that line denote a declining population and values above that line are increasing (modified from Anthony et al. 2006).

of the control of federal land managers (such as oceanic conditions in the case of Marbled Murrelets, competition from increasing Barred Owl (*Strix varia*) populations for Northern Spotted Owls, and management of forests in state or private ownership for both species) may also be important in determining the likelihood of species persistence. The FEMAT envisioned a monitoring program for other forest birds, but one was never implemented primarily due to competing demands for limited funding. Instead, managers rely on a variety of other shorter term studies to evaluate the status of birds associated with older forest.

Conclusion

Research data on the relative abundance of birds in relation to structural stage and forest attributes proved essential in refining a list of species associated with older forest and evaluating the likelihood of persistence of those species under a range of forest management alternatives. This knowledge helped craft the final design of the Northwest Forest Plan, which remains one of the world's most comprehensive attempts to conserve biological diversity. Research and monitoring have been essential to the adaptive management process, which is an inherent component of the forest plan (Haynes et al. 2006, Raphael 2006b). Although monitoring of the two federally listed species is ongoing, there remains a need to evaluate whether the plan has been successful in meeting the needs of other forest birds.

A Watershed Analysis for Establishing Local Population Objectives for Pacific-slope Flycatchers and a Suite of Mid- to Late-Successional Pacific Northwest Landbirds

Bob Altman, Michael T. Green, Barb Bresson, Erin Stockenberg, Daniel Casey, and Susannah Casey

Abstract

We provide an example of how modeling bird-habitat relationships with geospatial analyses can be used to assess the capacity of the landscape to establish local bird population objectives in support of Partners in Flight continental population objectives, and also provide an accounting tool for assessing the impact of forest management on bird populations. We initially focus on the process and outcomes for Pacific-slope Flycatchers (*Empidonax difficilis*) within the U.S. Forest Service boundaries of the Hamma Hamma watershed in western Washington. We then do the same analysis for a suite of mid- and late-successional focal bird species as an example of optimizing conservation efforts for several species at once. Our 30-year scenario of natural succession includes 10% harvest of the 61–80 year age class, and 100% thinning of the 41–60 year age class, in order to increase the populations of Pacific-slope Flycatchers by 12%, Winter Wrens (*Troglodytes troglodytes*) by 11%, Varied Thrushes (*Ixoreus naevius*) by 8%, and Townsend's Warblers (*Dendroica townsendi*) or Hermit Warblers (*Dendroica occidentalis*) by 3%.

Introduction

Forest land managers must balance the needs of a variety of biological and non-biological factors when making management decisions. Landscapes that have been designed and managed to meet these diverse needs result in an efficient use of resources. One of the potential management targets is bird conservation. A recent emphasis in landbird conservation is the modeling of bird populations and habitat relationships to provide quantitative habitat objectives. These habitat objectives are directly linked to bird population abundance objectives and provide the avian component of conservation design. One challenge for forest managers interested in bird conservation is designing optimal landscapes to meet the needs of multiple bird species. As an example of how this challenge can be addressed, we modeled bird-habitat relationships and conducted geospatial analyses in the 16,793 ha Hamma Hamma watershed in the Hood Canal Ranger District of the Olympic National Forest (Fig. 1) first for Pacific-slope Flycatchers (*Empidonax difficilis*) and then three mid- and late-successional forest focal bird species. The three additional species are Winter Wrens (*Troglodytes troglodytes*), Varied Thrushes (*Ixoreus naevius*), and Townsend's (*Dendroica townsendi*) or Hermit (*Dendroica occidentalis*) Warblers (these two species are treated together in this paper because of range overlap, hybridization, and difficulties with vocal identification).

Pacific-slope Flycatcher

Population objectives.—Partners in Flight (PIF) North American Landbird Conservation Plan (Rich et al. 2004) used range-wide Breeding Bird Survey (BBS) trend data (Sauer et al. 2008) to establish an ideal (i.e., not based on potential or capacity to achieve it) population abundance objective to maintain the continental population of Pacific-slope Flycatchers at the current level over the next 30 years. These continental population objectives were set to stimulate dialogue and action towards conservation of continental priority bird species. The expectation was that regional and local assessments would be conducted to establish habitat-based population abundance objectives at those scales that reflect the practical realities of those areas to contribute towards the continental objective. Often within a species range there is substantial variation in BBS trends from significantly declining to significantly increasing, and substantial variation in the problems and opportunities for trying to maintain or increase the species population. Thus, the variability of local and regional conditions and the projections of how those conditions might change over time, warrant a habitat-based approach to developing local or regional population objectives that are realistic within the context of current and projected future land uses.

Habitat relationships.—In western Washington, Pacific-slope Flycatchers are primarily associated

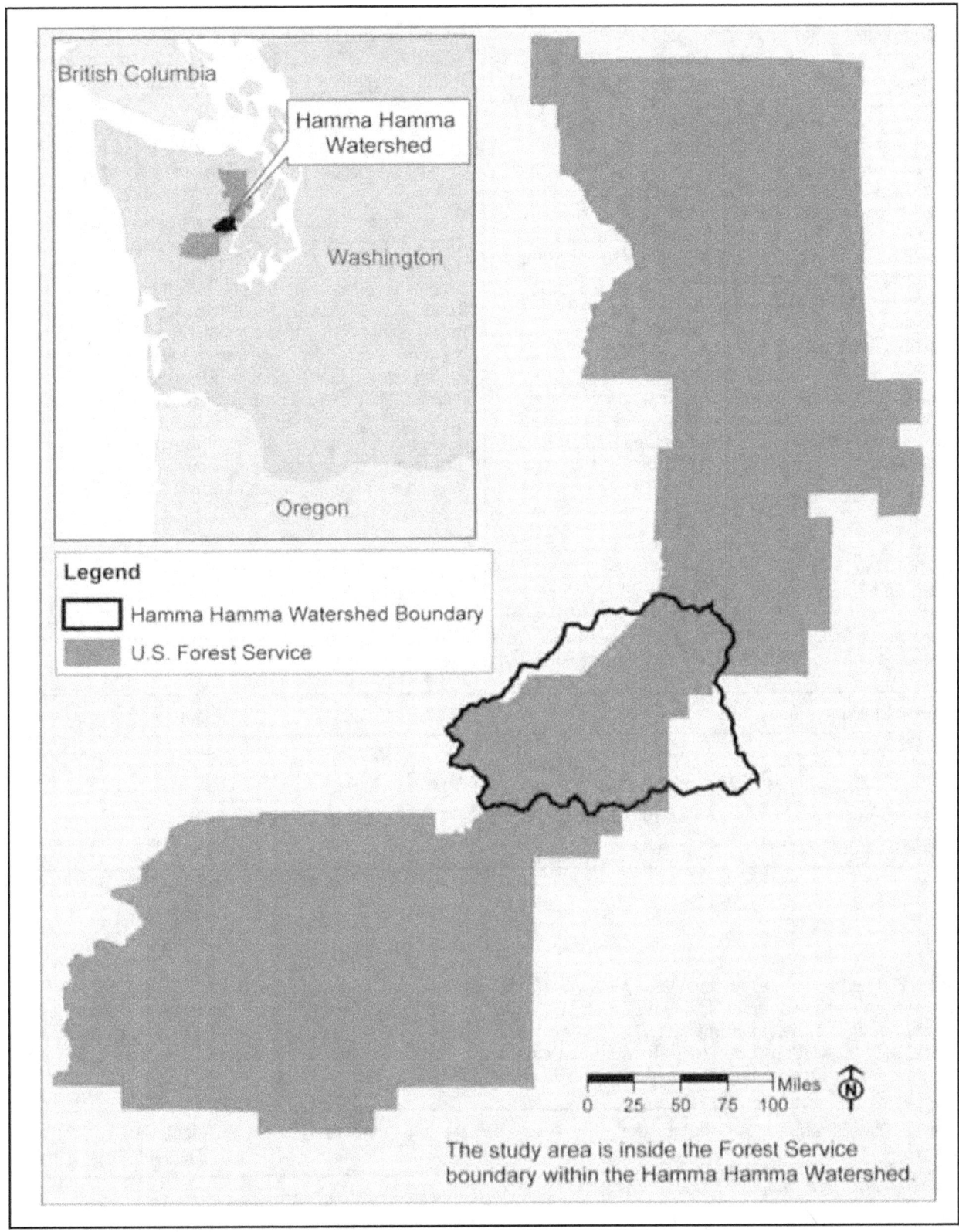

Figure 1. Hamma Hamma watershed, Hood Canal Ranger District, Olympic National Forest, Washington.

with mesic coniferous forest, mixed coniferous-deciduous forest, and especially deciduous forest (Leu 2000, Pearson and Manuwal 2001). Additionally, they are most abundant in late-successional forest (Manuwal 1991), and occur mostly at low to moderate elevations (generally <1250 m; Smith et al. 1997).

Vegetation classifications.—We used the Olympic National Forest Total Resource Inventory (TRI) GIS layer. This layer includes over 40 forest habitat classifications and six different forest age classifications. The only TRI classification in the Hamma Hamma watershed consistent with suitable breeding habitat for Pacific-slope Flycatchers is western hemlock (*Tsuga heterophylla*). Four of the six age-classes of forest were considered suitable habitat; 41–60 years (young forest), 61–80 years (young/mature forest), 81–160 years (mature forest), and > 160 years (old-growth forest).

Bird densities.—We assigned Pacific-slope Flycatcher density values to each suitable habitat classification based on studies that provided actual density estimates from spot-mapping or program DISTANCE (Thomas et al. 2003). We only used densities from the ecological region of the Hamma Hamma watershed (i.e., southwestern British Columbia, western Washington, and northwestern Oregon), and from the same habitat type (i.e., western hemlock) and age classes (Table 1).

Population estimates.—Using bird densities and area of suitable habitat by age class, we estimated the current population of Pacific-slope Flycatcher within the study area to be 11,293 birds (Table 2).

Future population projections.—We modeled the future population at 30-years to be consistent with the time frame used in the PIF Continental Plan for setting continental population objectives. We assumed both natural succession and forest management. Natural succession results in a gain in population because Pacific-slope Flycatcher densities increase in older forests (Table 2).

We used an example management scenario of 10% harvest (i.e., clear-cut) of young/mature forest (61–80 year age class) and 100% thinning of young forest (41–60 year age class) based on general knowledge of current forest management activities in the region. In our models, harvest results in an immediate and complete loss of habitat suitability (and birds) in harvested stands during our time frame of 30 years. Thinning results in an immediate reduction of the quality of the habitat for Pacific-slope Flycatchers (and hence densities of birds), although returns to original densities would be expected in the later half of our 30-year time frame

Table 1. Pacific-slope Flycatcher (*Empidonax difficilis*) density estimates by forest classification for the Hamma Hamma watershed on the Olympic National Forest, Washington. Density is the mean density (range) from various studies and is reported as birds ha-1 but equated to pairs ha-1 because the detections are almost always singing males and presumably maed birds since the studies were conducted during the breeding season. Sample size is the number of reported density estimates (BA).

Forest Classification	Years Old	Density (pairs ha-1)	Sample Size
Young Forest	41-60	0.27 (0.19-0.35)	8
Young/Mature Forest	61-80	0.70 (0.27-1.09)	9
Mature Forest	81-160	0.80 (0.37-1.11)	10
Old-Growth Forest	>160	1.09 (0.62-1.19)	6

Table 2. Pacific-slope Flycatcher (*Empidonax difficilis*) population estimates for the Hamma Hamma watershed on the Olympic National Forest, Washington. WH = western hemlock; numbers indicate the dominant age of the stand in years; 0 – 40 years are not presented because that age class is not considered suitable habitat. Population (# individuals) calculated by multiplying area of habitat x bird density x two (to account for the second individual of each pair in the population).

Forest Classification	Habitat (ha)	Bird Density (pairs ha-1)	Population (# individuals)[b]
WH 41-60	369	0.27	199
WH 61-80	1817	0.70	2544
WH 81-160	240	0.80	384
WH >160	3746	1.09	8166
Total			11,293

(Altman and Hagar 2006). To establish a single density estimate covering the changes over time, we used the percent difference of the cumulative mean density between thinned stands versus stands not thinned in four studies representing 1–24 years post-thinning (Artman 1990, Hagar et al. 1996, Muir et al. 2002, Hagar et al. 2004). This resulted in a mean density that was 30% less in thinned habitat, or a density of 0.19 birds ha^{-1}. When population losses from harvest and thinning are combined with population gains from natural succession, the outcome is a population of 12,600 birds (Table 3) or a gain of 1307 birds (approximately 12%).

Alternatives to increase the population.—We assessed two alternatives to increase the population. A change in our management scenario to include no thinning and no harvest results in modest population gains (255 birds or 2% for the no harvest and 125 birds or 1% for the no thinning). However, it is unrealistic on managed public lands to project no harvest and no thinning.

Another consideration is to increase suitability of existing habitat by increasing bird densities greater than the mean density we assumed. Two alternatives are to: 1) encourage mature deciduous tree growth in appropriate places by creating small openings or plantings; and 2) emphasize larger patches of forest because the species is considered a forest interior species with increased densities in larger patches (Rosenberg and Raphael 1986, Brand and George 2001, George and Brand 2002). In order to achieve significant gains in population from these alternatives they would have to be implemented extensively across the landscape, and that is simply unrealistic. Additionally, the time to achieve these habitat conditions is well beyond our 30-year time frame.

Optimization with a Suite of Focal Species

Our analysis so far assumes management in the Hamma Hamma watershed only for the habitat needs of Pacific-slope Flycatchers, an unlikely scenario because management for a single species is generally not conducted unless it is a federally-listed threatened or endangered species. Additionally, there are many other management considerations that would likely need to be applied to the region, including consideration of Late Successional Reserves (i.e., mature and old-growth forests designated for conservation under the Northwest Forest Plan; Forest Ecosystem Management Assessment Team 1993) and harvest targets for timber management, as well as management for other bird species of interest.

In the interest of developing a more inclusive and realistic model, we assessed the effects of this Pacific-slope Flycatcher management scenario on

Table 3. Pacific-slope Flycatcher (*Empidonax difficilis*) population projections in 30 years with natural succession and management (10% harvest of 61–80 year age class and 100% thinning of 41–60 year age class) in the Hamma Hamma watershed on the Olympic National Forest, Washington. WH = western hemlock; numbers indicate the dominant age of the stand in years. New habitat assumes equal distribution of hectares among age classes when adding 30 years (which moves old habitat into one or two new habitat age classes) thus proportioning of hectares into new age classes is necessary. Population (# individuals) calculated by multiplying area of habitat x bird density x two (to account for the second individual of each pair in the population).

Forest Classification	Old Habitat (ha)	New Habitat (ha)	Density (pairs ha-1)	Population (# individuals)
WH 0-20	819[a]			
WH 21-40	775[a]			
WH 41-60	369	798[b]	0.19[c]	303
WH 61-80	1817	573[d]	0.70	802
WH 81-160	240	2002[e]	0.80	3203
WH >160	3746	3804[f]	1.09	8292
Total				**12,600**

[a] Not considered suitable habitat, but presented because these numbers figure in the calculation of future suitable habitat due to natural succession.

[b] Calculated by adding 50% of the 21–40 year age class + 50% of the 0–20 year age class.

[c] Percent difference of the cumulative mean density between thinned versus unthinned in four studies (see text) representing 1–4 years post-thinning (i.e., 30% lower density in thinned) applied to the existing mean density in the 41–60 year age class.

[d] Calculated by adding 50% of the 41–60 year age class + 50% of the 21–40 year age class.

[e] Calculated by adding all of the 61–80 year age class (after 10% harvest) + 50% of the 41–60 year age class + 76% (prorated) of the existing 81 – 160 year age class that remains as 81 – 160.

[f] Calculated by adding all of the > 160 age class + 24% (prorated) of the 81–160 year age class that advances to > 160.

three other forest species to see whether or not we could maximize (optimize) bird conservation. The additional birds are focal species (Lambeck 1997) in the Oregon-Washington PIF Bird Conservation Plan (Altman 1999) that represent a suite of desired habitat conditions within mid- and late-successional forests including Winter Wrens (complex understory), Varied Thrushes (multi-layered midstory), and Townsend's and Hermit Warblers (high canopy cover). These four focal species complement Pacific-slope Flycatchers' habitat (deciduous tree component) and capture the desired habitat conditions of most bird species in mid- and late-successional forests.

Continental population objectives.—All four focal species are species of continental importance in the PIF Continental Plan, and all have objectives to maintain the current population abundance at the continental level over the next 30 years (Rich et al. 2004).

Habitat relationships.—Among all four bird species, suitable breeding habitat only occurs in stands > 40 years old, and includes four TRI habitat classifications; silver/noble fir (*Abies amabalis/procers*), western hemlock, mountain hemlock (*Tsuga mertensiana*), and silver fir/mountain hemlock. There were no forest classifications in which all four bird species occurred (i.e., the same habitat and age class). Winter Wrens had the broadest habitat range including all four habitats and all elevations; however, there are areas of overlap in habitat among the four species (Table 4).

Bird densities and population estimates.—For each focal species, we assigned density values for each forest type and age class as described earlier for Pacific-slope Flycatchers (Appendix). Existing population estimates were derived by multiplying bird densities by area of suitable habitat.

Future population projections.—We modeled the future population for each focal species under the same scenario as described earlier for Pacific-slope Flycatchers. We used the same method for calculating overall 30-year mean densities in the 41–60 year age class thinned stands as we did for Pacific-slope Flycatcher. The quantitative differences in mean densities between stands that were thinned and not thinned over the 30-year period were: Winter Wrens, a 21% higher density in thinned; Varied Thrushes, a 16% higher density in thinned; and Hermit and Townsend's Warblers, a 7% lower density in thinned. When population losses from harvest and losses or gains from thinning are combined with population gains from natural succession, the predicted outcome is population gains of 1724 (11.1%) for Winter Wrens, 433 (8%) for Varied Thrushes, and 71 (3%) for Hermit or Townsend's Warblers (Appendix).

Assessing impacts on bird populations.—In addition to establishment of population objectives, our bird-habitat modeling, geospatial analyses, and optimization provides forest managers a process for efficient bird conservation design and assessing outcomes of management on bird populations. We provide few example scenarios within the Hamma Hamma watershed that maximize bird conservation through natural succession, minimize the negative population impacts of harvest, and manage species-specific population losses and gains resulting from thinning (Table 5).

Discussion

Population objectives.—The future management options we described within the Forest Service lands of the Hamma Hamma watershed results in objectives to increase the population by approximately 12% for Pacific-slope Flycatchers, 11% for Winter Wrens, 8% for Varied Thrushes, and 3% for Hermit and Townsend's Warblers. These are modest gains over a 30-year period, but since much of this part of the watershed is already in late-successional forest there are limited opportunities for increasing populations of late-successional bird species. If the analyses were conducted for the entire watershed, the remainder of which is comprised of private forest lands and likely in much younger age classes, there would be more possibilities to increase populations with some

Table 4. Habitat compatibility among four focal species in the Hamma Hamma watershed on the Olympic National Forest, Washington.

Species Combinations	Habitats and Elevations
Winter Wrens and Hermit and Townsend's Warblers	Silver/noble fir < 500 m
Pacific-slope Flycatchers and Winter Wrens	Western hemlock < 500 m
Winter Wrens and Varied Thrushes	All habitats > 1250 m and mountain hemlock and silver fir/mountain hemlock 500–1250 m
Winter Wrens, Varied Thrushes, and Hermit and Townsend's Warblers	Silver/noble fir 500–1250 m
Pacific-slope Flycatchers, Winter Wrens, and Varied Thrushes	Western hemlock 500–1250 m

Table 5. Example management objectives to maximize bird focal species conservation in the Hamma Hamma watershed on the Olympic National Forest, Washington.

Management	Ideal Focal Species Scenario	Example Objective	Focal Species Rationale
Natural Succession	Manage where most species occur, where their densities are high, and where most habitat occurs	Allow succession to occur in western hemlock 500-1250 meters	Benefits 3 of the 4 species
Thinning	Conduct least where Pacific-slope Flycatchers and Hermit/Townsend's Warblers occur, and most where Winter Wrens and Varied Thrushes occur	Thin in silver/noble fir and in western hemlock >500 meters	Limits negative population effects on Pacific-slope Flycatchers and Hermit/Townsend's Warblers, while enhances positive population effects on Winter Wrens and Varied Thrushes
Harvest	Conduct where fewest number of species occur, and where their densities are low	Harvest in silver/noble fir > 1250 meters Harvest in western hemlock < 500 meters	Affects only 2 of 4 species including Varied Thrushes which has lowest densities Affects only 2 of 4 species and limits negative effects on Pacific-slope Flycatchers which has highest densities

targeted management for mid- and late-successional forests. Conversely, much of this land is intensively managed for timber production and harvested before achieving mid- to late-successional status, so opportunities for increasing populations would be negated to some degree by the realities of land ownership and management.

It is noteworthy that Pacific-slope Flycatchers, the species most negatively affected by thinning over a 30-year time frame, shows the highest population increase (i.e., the highest population objective). This is because it occurs in the highest densities of the four species, and its only suitable habitat, western hemlock, is the dominant forest type in the study area. Thus, despite losses in population due to thinning, it benefits greatly from the large amount of natural succession in western hemlock and the most birds per unit area in that habitat. This exemplifies the need to consider all management scenarios and long-term objectives, including natural succession, rather than just assessing short-term impacts based on a species response to one management activity.

Our analysis is presented as an example of how using geospatial data and bird-habitat data can be used to develop bird population objectives. These same types of analyses should be routinely done as part of forest planning throughout western Washington and elsewhere to determine cumulatively what a region can contribute towards the continental population objectives of these and other bird species.

Management impacts.—Our process of using bird-habitat data and geospatial analyses can be a valuable "accounting" tool for assessing management impacts directly on bird populations rather than indirectly on bird habitat. The results of the analyses allow for comparative accounting of impact on bird populations among alternatives, and thus can be used to advance strategic bird conservation. This tool has many additional potential applications for use in projects such as environmental assessments, land acquisition evaluations, and restoration proposals.

It is important to recognize that our example optimization analysis is not complete. Our example needs to be integrated with a similar analysis of a suite of early-successional focal bird species to balance their habitat needs and population objectives. Additionally, there are many non-bird considerations that would need to be applied. These comprehensive types of analyses will be necessary across regional landscapes not only to determine optimal bird conservation, but efficient management and conservation of all natural resources. Finally, we did not conduct an analysis of demographic data to provide complementary population objectives for primary population parameters such as reproduction, survivorship, or recruitment into the population. This should be done in concert with the analysis described herein for population abundance to provide population objectives for both primary and secondary population parameters.

Acknowledgments

Funding for this work was provided by the Bureau of Land Management, Oregon State Office. We thank Arvind O. Panjabi, C. John Ralph, Jaime L. Stephens, and an anonymous reviewer for comments on earlier drafts.

Appendix.

Existing and 30-year population estimates for Winter Wrens, Varied Thrushes, and Hermit and Townsend's Warblers with natural succession and management (10% harvest of 61-80 age class and 100% thinning of 41-60 age class) in the Hamma Hamma watershed on the Olympic National Forest, Washington. WH = western hemlock; SN = silver/noble fir; MH = mountain hemlock; SM = silver fir/mountain hemlock. Densities (pairs ha-1) are mean densities from reported studies (sample size). Densities without sample sizes were projected based on known densities from other age classes. Population (# individuals) calculated by multiplying area of habitat x bird density x two (to account for the second individual of each pair). Under Future Projections, New Habitat (ha) assumes equal distribution of hectares among age classes when adding 30 years which moves old habitat into one or two new habitat age classes; thus, proportioning of hectares into new age classes is necessary.

Forest Class	Habitat (ha)			Densities (pairs ha-1)			Population (# individuals)		
	Winter Wrens	Varied Thrushes	Hermit/ Townsend's Warblers	Winter Wrens	Varied Thrushes	Hermit/ Townsend's Warblers	Winter Wrens	Varied Thrush	Hermit/ Townsend's Warblers
Existing Conditions and Population Estimates									
WH 0-20	819.00[a]	785.00[a]							
WH 21-40	790.42[a]	750.42[a]							
WH 41-60	369.29	227.28		0.29 (8)	0.05 (12)		214.19	22.73	
WH 61-80	1826.86	778.23		0.38	0.14 (4)		1388.41	217.90	
WH 81-160	240.43	240.43		0.49 (9)	0.18 (11)		235.62	86.55	
WH >160	3848.74	3181.27		0.94 (5)	0.21 (8)		7235.63	1336.13	
SN 0-20	240.00[a]	240.00[a]	238.00						
SN 21-40	90.31[a]	90.31[a]	89.80						
SN 41-60	28.13	28.13	4.25	0.27 (2)	0.12 (2)	0.86 (14)	15.19	6.75	7.31
SN 61-80	744.51	744.06	686.53	0.39	0.28	0.78	580.72	416.67	1070.99
SN 81-160	92.51	92.51	92.47	0.55	0.30 (2)	0.67 (3)	101.76	55.51	123.91
SN >160	2615.31	2611.91	2522.79	0.72 (2)	0.47 (3)	0.29 (9)	3766.05	2455.20	1463.22
MH 61-80	108.88	108.88		0.45	0.28		97.99	60.97	
MH 81-160	232.32	232.32		0.59	0.31 (4)		274.14	144.04	
MH >160	972.85	972.85		0.77 (2)	0.47 (3)		1498.19	914.48	
SM 61-80	87.48	87.48		0.51	0.26		89.23	45.49	
SM 81-160				0.75 (4)	0.31 (4)				
Totals							15,497.12	5762.43	2665.43

Continued on next page

Continued from previous page

Forest Class	New Habitat (ha)			Densities (pairs ha-1)			Population (# individuals)		
	Winter Wrens	Varied Thrushes	Hermit/ Townsend's Warblers	Winter Wrens	Varied Thrushes	Hermit/ Townsend's Warblers	Winter Wrens	Varied Thrush	Hermit/ Townsend's Warblers
Future Projections of Habitat and Population Estimates									
WH 41-60	804.71[b]	767.71[b]		0.35[c]	0.06[c]		563.30	92.12	
WH 61-80	579.86[d]	488.85[d]		0.38	0.14 (4)		440.69	136.88	
WH 81-160	2011.55[e]	996.77[e]		0.49 (9)	0.18 (11)		1971.32	358.84	
WH >160	3906.44[f]	3238.97[f]		0.94 (5)	0.21 (8)		7344.11	1360.47	
SN 41-60	165.16[b]	165.16[b]	163.90[b]	0.33[c]	0.14[c]	0.80[c]	109.61	46.25	262.24
SN 61-80	59.22[d]	59.22[d]	47.03[d]	0.39	0.28	0.78	46.19	33.16	73.37
SN 81-160	754.43[e]	754.03[e]	690.28[e]	0.55	0.30 (2)	0.67 (3)	829.87	452.42	924.98
SN >160	2637.51[f]	2634.11[f]	2544.98[f]	0.72 (2)	0.47 (3)	0.29 (9)	3798.01	2476.06	1476.09
MH 61-80	54.44[d]	54.44[d]		0.45	0.28		49.08	30.49	
MH 81-160	274.56[e]	274.56[e]		0.59	0.31 (4)		323.98	170.23	
MH >160	1028.61[f]	1028.61[f]		0.77 (2)	0.47 (3)		1584.06	966.89	
SM 61-80	43.74[d]	43.74[d]		0.51	0.26		43.74	22.75	
SM 81-160	78.73[e]	78.73[e]		0.75 (4)	0.31 (4)		118.10	48.81	
Totals							**17,221.46**	**6195.37**	**2736.68**
Number of birds gained in population							1724.34	432.94	71.25
Percent population gain (i.e., population objective)							11.1%	7.5%	2.7%

[a] Not considered suitable habitat, but area presented because these numbers figure in the calculation of future suitable habitat due to natural succession.

[b] Calculated by adding 50% of the 21 – 40 year age class + 50% of the 0 – 20 year age class.

[c] Densities are different from existing conditions densities due to thinning. Calculation is the percent difference of the cumulative mean density between thinned versus unthinned in four studies (see text) representing 1 – 24 years post-thinning (i.e., 30% lower density in thinned) applied to the existing mean density in the 41– 60 year age class.

[d] Calculated by adding 50% of the 41 – 60 year age class + 50% of the 21 – 40 year age class.

[e] Calculated by adding all of the 61 – 80 year age class (after 10% harvest) + 50% of the 41 – 60 year age class + 76% (prorated) of the existing 81-160 year age class that remains as 81 – 160.

[f] Calculated by adding all of the > 160 year age class + 24% (prorated) of the 81–160 year age class

Demographic Monitoring, Modeling, and Management of Landbird Populations in Forests of the Pacific Northwest: An Application of the MAPS Dataset

M. Philip Nott, and Nicole L. Michel

Abstract

Pacific Northwest forests support over a hundred breeding landbird species (including many Neotropical migrants) in a variety of forested, meadow, shrub, and riparian habitats. With the need for increased management to both maintain the health of those habitats and reduce the risk of wildfire managers need tools to assess the effect of their management. Additionally, these habitats and the birds that breed in them face increasingly variable environmental conditions due to recent and extreme fluctuations in weather patterns driven by cyclical phenomena associated with the Pacific (e.g. the El Nino Southern Oscillation) and Atlantic (e.g. the North Atlantic Oscillation) oceans. Demographic monitoring of the avifauna can help determine the proximal causes of population change (i.e., whether changes are linked to survival rates and/or to reproductive effort). Survival rates are likely mostly influenced by conditions during the non-breeding season whereas reproductive effort is likely most influenced by conditions just prior to and during the breeding season and by the pattern and health of the forested landscapes.

The Institute for Bird Populations, monitored 21 landbird species in six national forests and calculated their survival rates and annual reproductive indices. Of these 21 species, we identified 13 species of conservation concern that were listed in federal, regional, and state conservation plans. For these 13 species, we constructed species-landscape models from which we formulated management guidelines to maintain or create landscapes that support healthy productive populations. GIS-based simulations can be used to generate post-management landscapes, the spatial statistics of which can be used to populate multiple species-landscape models. In this way, managers can assess the effects of alternate management scenarios (or natural disturbances) on breeding landbird populations.

Introduction

The U.S. Forest Service Pacific Northwest Region manages 19 national forests that provide timber, forage for cattle and wildlife, and numerous recreational opportunities. These and similar activities on lands surrounding national forests affect avian communities through alteration or removal of their preferred habitats.

In 1993, the Pacific Northwest Forest Plan emerged for coordinating forest management actions with federal agencies and state, local, and tribal governments across Oregon, Washington, and California. The plan includes strategies for adaptive forest management, conservation and restoration of riparian habitat, and the protection of sensitive species on federal forestlands (U.S. Department of Agriculture and U.S. Department of the Interior 1994a).

In addition, Partners in Flight formulated avian conservation plans (Rich et al. 2004) at the federal, regional, and state levels that list species of conservation concern and the critical habitats that they require to successfully breed. These plans call for adaptive management guidelines to maintain or improve habitats for species of conservation concern.

It is essential, therefore, to construct appropriately scaled ecological models that can quantify the effects of changing landscape pattern and structure on avian population dynamics. Such models could be used by land managers as decision-making tools to enable them to predict the effects of proposed forest management activities on avian demographics, including population densities, population trajectories, and reproductive success.

Developing Species-Habitat Models from Monitoring Avian Productivity and Survivorship Data

The Institute for Bird Populations (IBP), through collaboration with (and funding from) U.S. Forest Service, Pacific Northwest Region Six established

36 demographic monitoring stations under the Monitoring Avian Productivity and Survivorship (MAPS; DeSante et al. 1995, DeSante and Nott 2001) program (Fig. 1; Table 1). Since 1992, these stations have effectively monitored 21 landbird species on six national forests of the Pacific Northwest. Of these 21 species, we constructed species-landscape models for 13 species.

We collected breeding season mist-netting and banding data from 36 constant-effort monitoring stations (Nott et al. 2005). In 1992, six stations were established on each of six national forests (Fig. 1; Table 1): two in Washington, and four in Oregon. We collated and analyzed banding data (1992 - 2001) from each station to obtain study-wide, forest-specific, and station-specific demographic parameters for 21 species (Nott et al. 2005). Of these, species-landscape models were constructed for 13 species of management concern whose demographics could be modeled (minimum of eight stations each capturing 2.5 adult birds per year) and

that were also included in federal, regional, or state conservation plans.

We defined two sets of MAPS stations in this investigation. A "Northwest Forests" set included those 36 MAPS stations operated on national forest lands with the financial and logistical support of the U.S. Forest Service Region 6 (Fig. 1; Table 1). A more spatially extensive "Pacific Northwest Regional" set (not shown) included the Northwest Forest set as well as 150+ "independent" stations operated by public agencies, academic institutions, private organizations, and individual bird banders. We used the Pacific Northwest Regional dataset to correct the raw MAPS data for missed banding effort (Nott and DeSante 2002a) as defined by the MAPS constant-effort mist netting protocol (DeSante et al. 2010) and effort correction algorithm. The diurnal- and seasonal-correction models (Nott and DeSante 2002b) were then applied to the less extensive Northwest Forests dataset to determine the forest-specific avian demographics subsequently

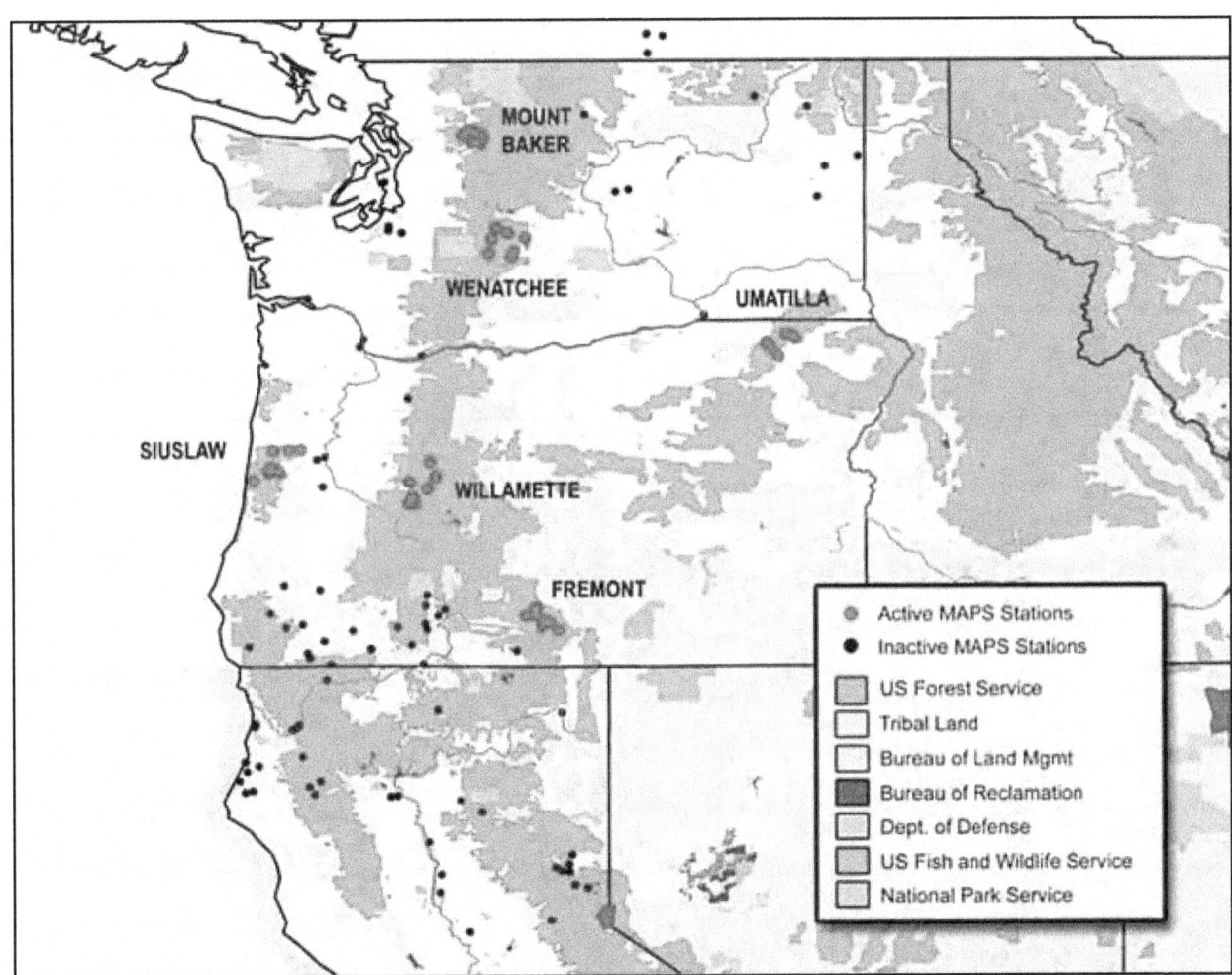

Figure 1. Clusters of MAPS stations (red circles) located on six named national forests (green) in Washington (2), and Oregon (4), where landbird species of conservation concern have been monitored by the Institute for Bird Populations (IBP) since 1992. Other MAPS stations that have been active for four or more years but not operated by IBP are shown as black dots. MAPS stations are superimposed upon federally-managed lands as denoted by yellow (Tribal Land), light tan (Bureau of Land Management), brown (Bureau of Reclamation), gray (Department of Defense), green (Forest Service), orange (Fish and Wildlife Service), and blue (National Park Service).

Table 1. The direction of the forest-wide trend for each of 13 species (eight Neotropical and five short-distance migrants) of regional conservation concern is indicated as decreasing (-) or increasing (+), and significance is indicated by multiple plus or minus characters (e.g. + = non-significant, ++ = $0.05 \leq P < 0.10$, +++ = $0.01 \leq P < 0.05$). The species of forest-specific management concern for which adult populations are declining significantly at one or more stations are shown shaded. For each national forest, the number of species of management concern (declining significantly at one or more stations) is given with the numbers of species with declining or increasing trends.

Species of regional conservation concern	Baker	Wenatchee	Umatilla	Willamette	Siuslaw	Fremont
Neotropical migrants						
Hammond's Flycatchers	-	+	—	+++		++
"Western" Flycatchers	-			-	—	+
Warbling Vireos	+	-	—	+		-
Swainson's Thrushes	++	+	—	+	+	
MacGillivray's Warblers	-	-	—	-		+
Wilson's Warblers	+	+	-	+++	+	-
Chipping Sparrows		-	—			
Lincoln's Sparrows	—		-	-		-
Short-distance migrants						
Chestnut-backed Chickadees	-	+++		-	-	
Winter Wrens	-		+++	++	-	
Song Sparrows	+	—		+++	+	
Dark-eyed Juncos	-	++	—	-		++
Pine Siskins		+	-	—		-
Total management concern	3	4	8	4	3	2
Total declining	6	5	9	6	3	4
Total increasing	4	6	1	6	3	4

used to parameterize landscape management models for birds of management concern. This process resulted in station- and species-specific annual numbers of adult and young birds. Reproductive success was expressed as the ratio of young to adults.

For each species of management concern, we analyzed MAPS banding data and combined demographic estimates with five regional spatial datasets: USGS National Land Cover Dataset (Vogelmann et al. 2001), USFS Region 6 canopy cover, USGS National Elevation Dataset (NED), Streamnet, and the USFS Forest Health Protection Aerial Survey (McConnell et al. 2000). From these we constructed landscape-scale (1000's of hectares) "species-landscape" models that describe demographic parameters as functions of the land cover (e.g. coniferous cover), canopy cover, edge type (e.g. forest-grassland), topography, water features (e.g. permanent stream density), and defoliation indices that represent the frequency and intensity of spatial pest outbreak data.

These species-landscape models can be used to predict the likely effect of forest management on adult population density and reproductive success for multiple species.

Management Goals

Forest management can change landscape patterns and structures that in turn can change avian diversity and local population trajectories (Mitchell et al. 2006). The species-landscape models provide tools that allow managers to assess the effects of management on species of conservation concern. In order to validate the models we must also, where possible, monitor the "effectiveness" of that management.

Accordingly, the next stage in the adaptive management cycle was to identify stations at which particular management could be applied that I expect to benefit species of conservation concern and to reorganize our network of monitoring stations to monitor the effectiveness of past or future management. In 2004 - 2005, we discontinued five stations and reestablished them in other parts of the forest to better monitor species of conservation concern, and measure the effects of thinning practices on their avian populations by locating new stations in similarly treated forests. We continue to operate the remaining 30 stations as control stations; they effectively monitor a number of species of concern in areas that are not managed.

Monitoring Regime

We used the MAPS monitoring protocol (DeSante et al. 2008). Each station consists of 10 nets located in the same place each year and, every ten days for three months, opened for six hours following sunrise. Birds are identified to species, age, and sex and marked with a federal band; in addition, morphometric (e.g. wing length, weight, etc.) and molt pattern data were recorded (DeSante et al. 2008).

Response to Management

Analyses of the demographic data revealed the direction and significance in adult population trends from MAPS data pooled by two national forests in Washington (Mount Baker and Wenatchee), and four in Oregon. Few stations were affected by nearby management during the period 1992 - 2001, so we can assume that these trends (Table 1) are the result of species response to historical (pre-1992) management or prevailing abiotic conditions. We hypothesized that the density and reproductive success of the species breeding there are a response to the landscape pattern resulting from historical management at the level of the landscape surrounding each MAPS station. By quantifying these responses we can construct models that can be used to reverse the declines.

Results of Models

The species-landscape models can be used to predict the likely effect of forest management on adult population density and reproductive success for multiple species. For example, the models can be used in the following manner to assess the effect of small clear cut:

(1) Select a 2 km radius of the landscape centered on the proposed cut.

(2) Gather relevant spatial statistics (to populate parameters of each model (e.g. percent cover of deciduous forest) using FragStats (McGarigal and Marks 1995) or equivalent.

(3) Estimate pre-management numbers of birds and reproductive indices.

(4) Simulate proposed management in multiple layers of a GIS application.

(5) Repeat spatial analysis to populate parameters of each model (repeat 2).

(6) Estimate post-management numbers of birds and reproductive indices.

(7) Compare pre- and post-management predictions of population density and reproduction to assess the impact of the proposed management on each species.

Adjustments to the simulated management can be made to selectively benefit one or more species or guild. For instance, to minimize the effect of clear-cutting (e.g. 100 ha of 1250 ha) upon species that requires large forest patches (e.g. Swainson's Thrush) you might cut a single 100 ha block and orient that cut to leave the largest uniformly shaped contiguous patch of low canopy cover coniferous forest possible. However, to maximize habitat for a species that prefers forest-shrub edge habitat many small narrow cuts should be made. In this way the models can be applied to multiple species and act as decision-making tools for managers to create or maintain high quality breeding habitat for species of regional or local conservation concern. Similarly, these models can be used to assess the consequences of proposed management upon local avifauna, or used in a "what if" sense to formulate management plans that maximize the benefits to multiple species. Continued monitoring of demographic performance measures (Nott and Morris 2007) in managed and unmanaged areas provides the ability to assess the efficacy of management or track the consequences of natural disturbances.

We summarize the general interpretations of species landscape models for each species and demographic for which statistically significant and interpretable models emerged. Overall, selected models for forest-dwelling species suggest that management plans should aim to conserve large areas of contiguous forest, upwards of 900 ha (72%), in a 2 km radius landscape covering 1250 ha. Within those forested areas, canopy cover, as well as the density of undergrowth and ground cover, should be managed in a manner consistent with published habitat management procedures for each target species. Riparian, deciduous, and edge habitat also emerged as important components of several species' habitat requirements.

Hammond's Flycatchers (Empidonax hammondii).—To maintain healthy and productive Hammond's Flycatcher populations, land managers should create a shifting mosaic of successional or low canopy cover habitat (covering 10 – 20% of the landscape) within extensive stands of uniformly shaped coniferous forest or woodland covering 80-90% of the landscape. Because reproductive success responds negatively to stream density, such management would best be applied to the drier higher elevation (600 - 1800 m) coniferous stands.

"Western" *Flycatcher* - The term "Western" Flycatcher refers to the occurrence of Pacific-slope (*Empidonax difficilis*) or Cordilleran (*Empidonax occidentalis*) flycatchers which cannot be distinguished from one another in the "hand" where their ranges overlap. "Western" Flycatchers as a group are sensitive to proximal edges (i.e., patch size) of coniferous habitat; smaller patch sizes might result in higher risk of nest predation and parasitism (Robinson et al. 1995). The numbers of young and reproductive success are higher at those stations associated with a high total core area of coniferous forest habitat totaling 72% of the landscape. Large tracts of old-growth forests (large core areas of coniferous forest) and dry-upland and riparian sites (thinner canopy and some mixed habitats) are beneficial to the reproductive success of "Western" Flycatchers.

Warbling Vireos (Vireo gilvus).—Warbling Vireos are associated with large tracts of coniferous forest, and with forest-successional and forest-grassland edge components. This suggests that creation of regeneration gaps could create productive habitat. However, the pattern of the logging may be important. The results suggest that at high elevations, large tracts of open coniferous forest interspersed with larger patches of successional habitat create good habitat for successful breeding.

Chestnut-backed Chickadees.—Chestnut-backed Chickadees are best managed through the creation or maintenance of open (thin-canopied) forest and forest-successional habitat edge, especially at higher elevations where pest damage was high. However, extensive riparian habitat, as reflected by stream density, was associated with increasing trends in the numbers of young and with reproductive success.

Other research suggests that pest infestation is a natural process that benefits bird populations (Torgersen et al. 1990, Crawford and Jennings 1989); while increased magnitude and extent of damage due to several species of bark beetle at higher elevations is likely a result of recent climate change and results in reducing the core area of forest and thinning canopy cover (Raffa et al. 2008). Our results show strong positive correlations between Chestnut-backed Chickadee demographics and elevation (spatial mean), the extent of successional habitat, and cumulative bark beetle damage.

Winter Wrens (Troglodytes troglodytes).—Higher populations and greater reproductive success of Winter Wrens were associated with large areas of evergreen forests. However, population sizes and reproductive success seem to be increasing over time in areas that were classified as thinner forest with successional habitat and a deciduous component. These results suggest that the best way to manage for Winter Wrens would be to maintain large uniformly shaped patches of thinner-canopy evergreen forests in stream-dense areas.

In addition, smaller patches of mixed or deciduous forests (associated with riparian areas and covering greater than 10% of the area) should be maintained.

Swainson's Thrushes (Catharus ustulatus).— Within coniferous forests, adult populations of Swainson's Thrushes required large patches (representing 10% or more of the landscape) of dense, low-elevation, deciduous and mixed-deciduous forests, with high canopy cover (i.e. mature lowland forests). However, numbers of young and increased reproductive success benefit from large patches (> 16% of the landscape) of more open deciduous and mixed habitat forests. The selection of highly correlated core area variables in these models supports previous findings of "edge sensitivity" for this species (Brand and George 2001). This emphasizes the need to conserve large tracts of contiguous forest in lowland areas where moister forests and riparian areas occur. The presence of grassland and successional habitat is deleterious to population dynamics. These results suggest that the riparian management, currently being implemented across the region, should lead to increases in Swainson's Thrush populations.

Inspection of the landscape data associated with the 25 MAPS stations used in Swainson's Thrush analyses reveals that coniferous forest was the dominant habitat type covering 50-90% of the 1250 hectares within a 2-kilometer radius of each station. Deciduous and mixed forest coverage, combined, accounted for up to 500 hectares (approx. 40%) of the remaining areas (e.g. station 11166) and averaged 13% of the cover. The coverage of successional habitat was consistently under 35 hectares (approx. 3%) except for stations 11143 (~9%) in Mount Baker N.F., 11154 (~40%), 11155 (~15%), and 11156 (~35%) in Umatilla N.F. We reported statistically significant correlations between demographics and landscape variables. At this sampling level ($n = 25$) two-tailed critical values of Pearson's correlation coefficient (r) lie at 0.337 ($P < 0.10$), 0.462 ($P < 0.05$) and 0.505 ($P < 0.01$). Figure 2 shows the forest fragmentation patterns associated with three Willamette MAPS stations; a fragmented high elevation station where thrushes' adult abundance and reproductive index were low; two lower elevation stations which were less fragmented and supported higher abundances and productivity levels.

MacGillivray's Warblers (Oporornis tolmiei).— MacGillivray's Warblers at higher elevations are best managed by maintaining large patches of successional habitat interspersed among low to medium canopy cover coniferous forest. Such a coarsely grained habitat should feature extensive successional habitat-forest edge. Although no strong correlations were found between stream density (indicative of the extent of riparian or meadow habitat) and demographic variables, stream density was generally high at the stations included in this study.

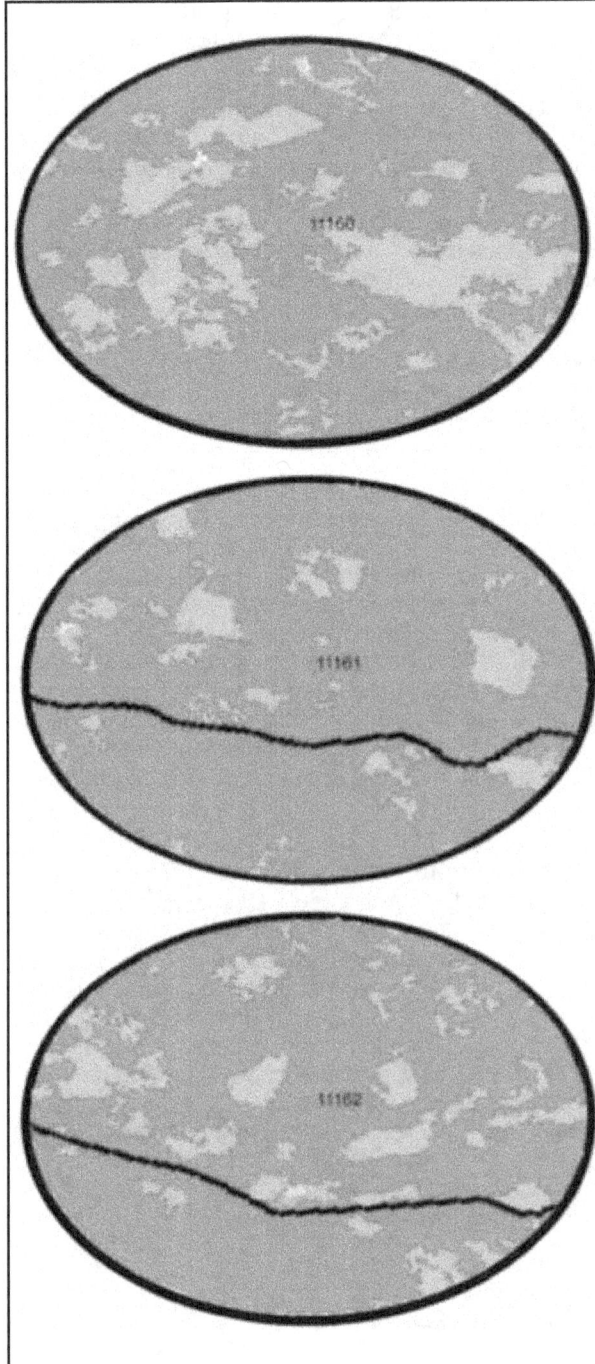

Figure 2. Aerial land cover images of 2 km radius (oval due to projection) landscapes derived from the National Land Cover Dataset (2001), associated with three MAPS stations that monitor Swainson's Thrush on Willamette NF. The forested (green) landscape surrounding the Clear Cut (#11160) station is more fragmented by shrub/successional habitat (tan) than that surrounding the stations Major Prairie (#11161), and Brock Creek (#11162). The latter two stations are at ~700m elevation and support stable and abundant adult population (10 and 13 adults per year, respectively) with high productivity indices (0.15 and 0.29, respectively), whereas Clear Cut at ~1300m elevation supports half the adult abundance (6 adults) with a productivity index of only 0.06.

Wilson's Warblers (Wilsonia pusilla).—Adult Wilson's Warblers abundance are most closely associated with deciduous habitats with successional habitat edge. However, the models also suggest that reproductive success was higher in successional habitats where the adults were less common. Therefore, riparian management zones do not appear to be as important to Wilson's Warblers as extensive high canopy cover deciduous forests. If riparian management zones include areas of deciduous forest, we predict that they will be beneficial to this species. We recommend the maintenance of high canopy cover deciduous or mixed forest in excess of 60% of the landscape and narrow successional habitat cover in excess of 4%.

Chipping Sparrows (Spizella passerina).—Chipping Sparrow models were weak but suggested that the maintenance of a coarse grained, heterogeneous forested landscape featuring larger patches of successional habitat and grassland should benefit Chipping Sparrow populations.

Song Sparrows (Melospiza melodia).—Song Sparrows appear to be edge-sensitive; thus, maintaining or creating large patches of low canopy cover evergreen forest in stream-dense areas should benefit adult and young populations and lead to high reproductive success. The results also suggest that defoliation events may help create suitable habitat for Song Sparrows by thinning the canopy. The extent of successional habitat should be held at less than 3%. It is possible that mechanical canopy thinning may also benefit Song Sparrow populations. Grazing exclusion and creek restoration will help restore higher elevation habitat of Song Sparrows.

Lincoln's Sparrows (Melospiza lincolnii).— Maintaining coarse grained habitat heterogeneity (meadow and successional) among high elevation moist coniferous forests is beneficial to Lincoln's Sparrow populations. At high elevations, frequent natural disturbances such as defoliation events may be responsible for the development of dense scrubby patches and edge habitats where Lincoln's Sparrows prefer to breed. Adults responded negatively to grassland area but young responded positively. Larger patches appear to represent better quality habitat in which individuals produce more offspring, whereas smaller patches are available to non-breeders or less fit individuals. This pattern fits an ideal despotic distribution which is commonly associated with the population dynamics of sparrows and other species (Moller 1991).

Dark-eyed Juncos (Junco hyemalis).—Maintaining coarse grained heterogeneity among drier, higher elevation coniferous forests benefits Dark-eyed Juncos. At high elevations, frequent natural disturbances such as defoliation events may be responsible for the development of dense scrubby patches and edge habitats where Dark-eyed Juncos populations appear to thrive. However, some populations thrived in areas where a mosaic of larger regeneration cuts had been created.

Pine Siskins (Spinus pinus).—Maintaining large contiguous (low levels of fragmentation) tracts of drier, high-elevation, coniferous forests is beneficial to Pine Siskins. Although populations declined at 11 of 13 stations they declined slower at stations dominated by high canopy cover forest. Interestingly, cumulative pest damage was significantly ($P < 0.05$) higher, by a factor of approximately 2.4, among the stations used in the Pine Siskins study than they were at the other 23 stations. Possibly, canopy cover reduction by insects helped cause the declines.

Conclusion

Healthy productive populations of 13 species of management concern depend upon differing landscape-scale factors. Some species, like Hammond's Flycatchers, depend upon the presence of contiguous coniferous forest with varying degrees of canopy cover. Other species, such as "Western" Flycatchers and Winter Wrens, depend upon sensitive forested riparian habitats. At higher elevations moist forest-meadow complexes are critical to species like MacGillivray's Warblers, and Lincoln's and Song sparrows. Also, at higher elevations, forests affected by defoliating insects and beetles appear to benefit Chestnut-backed Chickadees, Song Sparrows, and Dark-eyed Juncos reproductive success.

At higher elevations, a coarse-grained, habitat heterogeneity of forest, successional-shrubland, and grassland-meadow occurs naturally. This provides quality breeding habitat for several species including Chipping Sparrows and Pine Siskins. Habitat edges in these and other managed landscapes are ecologically important components in the population dynamics of several species. More importantly, specific pairs of habitats that make an edge may be a preferred habitat component. For example, Warbling Vireo reproductive success responded positively to forest-successional and forest-grassland edges. Other species, including Swainson's Thrushes and Chestnut-backed Chickadees, responded negatively to forest-grassland edge.

In this study, long-term demographic monitoring and species-landscape modeling have revealed important ecological relationships for demographics among 13 species of conservation concern. We can use these models to predict the effects of proposed forest management on populations of multiple breeding species, thereby providing useful decision-making tools. Furthermore, it is possible to spatially extend these models to map potential habitat for a particular species and forest type throughout an entire forest.

As monitoring continues on the newly established (and/or managed) stations through future breeding seasons, we will begin to compare observed numbers with predictions of my models and be able to validate this approach. A similar study, based on data collected from a network of stations located on Department of Defense lands in the eastern and south-central U. S., is used to predict the effects of management (Nott and Michel 2005). Recently, decision support tools were provided online for both the Department of Defense network (Nott and Chambers 2008) and this study (Nott and Kaschube 2007).

Finally, there are factors affecting the productivity and survival of forest birds that have nothing to do with management actions, especially shifting climates and regional variation in weather patterns, effects that are being detected globally (Root et al. 2003). The data used in this study were also used to reveal that climate and weather are strong influences upon avian population dynamics in the Pacific Northwest (Nott et al. 2002) and may mask the effects of habitat management on avifauna.

To remove the bias of climate and/or weather, it is important to quantify such relationships, especially in the light of global warming. In some regions it is increasingly valuable to quantify the variable patterns of precipitation and temperature. These influences can act directly upon the birds, for example, extreme weather on the breeding grounds, wintering grounds, or during migration, may reduce survival probabilities. In the longer term, assemblages of tree and understory plant species, and the invertebrate populations they support, will inevitably shift. These shifts will pose great conservation challenges to current and future managers of forested landscapes.

Acknowledgments

We thank the U.S. Forest Service Region 6, the National Fish and Wildlife Foundation, and the Pacific Coast Joint Venture for financial support. We also thank Barb Bresson and all my present and past contacts on the Mount Baker/Snoqualmie, Wenatchee, Umatilla, Siuslaw, Willamette, and Fremont national forests for logistic support, and all the IBP biologists and interns who have collected and verified these MAPS data over the past 16 years. This is Contribution Number 376 of The Institute for Bird Populations.

Integrating Avian Monitoring into Forest Management: Pine-Hardwood and Aspen Enhancement on the Lassen National Forest

Ryan D. Burnett

Abstract

The composition and structure of western North America forests have been altered by more than a century of fire suppression, timber harvest, and grazing. These management practices in the Sierra Nevada Mountains of California have shifted the competitive balance in favor of shade tolerant conifers over shade intolerant hardwoods such as black oak (*Quercus kelloggii*) and aspen (*Populus tremuloides*). Results from our previous monitoring in the Lassen National Forest, identified pine-oak (*Pinus-Quercus* species) and aspen habitat as among the most species rich avian habitats in the region. PRBO Conservation Science and the Lassen National Forest are collaborating to design and monitor both pine-oak and aspen enhancement projects across two ranger districts. These projects are intended to provide conditions that promote hardwood growth and recruitment and ensure the long term persistence of these habitat components on the landscape. Monitoring is a key element of these efforts and is occurring pre- and post-project implementation. Preliminary results have already been incorporated into project designs to benefit avian species that may have been negatively affected by other management objectives including grazing and fire suppression. Monitoring is also being used to set more specific quantitative objectives that can be used to evaluate the effectiveness of future projects. PRBO Conservation Science continues to work with the staffs of local U.S. Forest Service offices to find the most appropriate and efficient avenues for incorporating our results to guide future management and ensure the impetus for habitat enhancement continues.

Introduction

The species composition and structure of forests in western North America have been altered in the last century. The primary forces behind these changes are believed to be fire suppression and timber harvest practices (Minnich et al. 1995, Chang 1996, Stephenson 1999, Taylor 2000). Human-mediated shifts in the competitive balance of these vast and complex forest ecosystems can result in the widespread loss of unique and ecologically valuable habitat attributes upon which wildlife depend (Hejl 1994). In the mixed conifer forests that dominate the Sierra Nevada Mountains of California, these management practices have led to an increase in shade tolerant white fir (*Abies concolor*) and incense cedar (*Calocedrus deccurrens*) and declines in shade intolerant ponderosa and sugar pines (*P. ponderosa* and *P. lambertiana*) and hardwoods such as black oak (*Quercus kelloggii*) (Vankat and Major 1978, Parsons and Benedetti 1979, Minnich et al. 1995).

Similar to black oak, the persistence and vigor of aspen (*Populus tremuloides*) communities have been negatively affected by conifer encroachment that has occurred unchecked due to fire suppression (Mueggler 1985, Bartos 2001, Jones et al. 2005). In addition to conifer encroachment, the health and persistence of aspen can be negatively affected by grazing (Mueggler 1985). As a result, the health of aspen stands has deteriorated and their extent throughout western North America has been reduced by at least 50% and possibly as much as 96% (Bartos 2001). In the absence of natural processes such as fire, without management intervention, the health and the long-term persistence of aspen in the west are threatened (Kay 1997).

A key to developing a successful plan for managing large ecosystems is prioritizing habitat types in which to focus restoration actions. Structural diversity and black oak are positively correlated with avian diversity in mixed conifer forest in the Sierra Nevada (Beedy 1981, Airola and Barrett 1985). Avian monitoring conducted by PRBO Conservation Science (PRBO) in the Lassen region from 1997 – 2002 also identified mixed conifer forest with a hardwood component as supporting greater avian diversity than white-fir dominated mixed conifer forest that lacked hardwoods (Burnett and Humple 2003). The abundance and diversity of avian communities in aspen habitats in western forests has been documented (Flack 1976, Mills et al. 2000, Richardson and Heath 2005). Thus, with their value to birds, limited extent on the landscape, and current threats facing them, PRBO recommended aspen and pine-oak (*Pinus-Quercus species*) habitat enhancement as priorities for restoration action in the northern Sierra Nevada and southern Cascades of California.

In 2003, PRBO was approached by the Almanor Ranger District (ARD) of the Lassen National Forest to provide specific design considerations from an avian perspective on a 400 hectare pilot pine-oak restoration project. The following year, the ARD and the Eagle Lake Ranger District (ELRD) provided funding for PRBO to develop and implement an adaptive management-based avian monitoring program to evaluate and help guide future pine-oak and aspen habitat enhancement activities. Additional partners include the Aspen Delineation Project, University of California, Davis, and University of California Integrated Hardwood Range Management Program.

The U.S. Forest Service is emphasizing monitoring as part of an adaptive management ecological-based approach to forest management in the Sierra Nevada (Sierra Nevada Forest Plan Amendment 2004). As pine-oak and aspen enhancement are relatively new management practices in the region, monitoring and an adaptive management strategy are critical to providing managers with scientific results to help guide and evaluate such projects.

Avian monitoring is considered an excellent tool for providing feedback on the effects of land management actions (Temple and Wiens 1989, Hutto 1998, Burnett et al. 2005). Numerous avian species of management interest are associated with hardwood habitats in the Sierra Nevada and can provide information on the structure and function of ecological systems. These factors, along with concerns over widespread declines of Neotropical migratory birds (Finch and Stangel 1993), ensure bird monitoring of forest management is exceedingly relevant.

The primary goals of this project are to use a suite of avian focal species to help guide and evaluate Forest Service projects intended to stop the loss of aspen and shade intolerant pine and black oak components of mixed conifer forests.

Specifically, the pine-oak project was designed to:
(1) Reduce the overall amount of encroaching white fir;

(2) Where feasible establish ponderosa and sugar pines as the dominant conifers;

(3) Provide the conditions that enhance the health and increase the presence of black oak in treated stands over time.

These objectives include maintaining a minimum cover averaged across the stand of 30% oak and 30% conifer, with a maximum 10% overlap of canopies with approximately 20% of the stand in small openings. Pre-treatment stand conditions vary, but generally canopy closure is between 50–70% and dominated by white fir with a few sites still containing substantial oak cover and understory shrub components.

Specific objectives of the aspen enhancement are to improve site conditions for and promote the health and expansion of aspen clones by stimulating regeneration and increasing the vigor of existing stems. As with the pine-oak sites, pre-treatment conditions at aspen sites vary. However, most aspen stands are shaded by overtopping white fir and pine and have little to no regeneration in the understory. Unlike pine-oak enhancement, aspen treatments require converting sites back to an aspen dominated plant community from the heavily encroached conifer conditions that have developed over the past 100 years. Thus, current prescriptions involve removing the vast majority of conifers in and around remnant aspen stands, and where necessary, fencing stands to eliminate the negative impacts of grazing on recovering aspen. A detailed summary of prescriptions, pre-treatment conditions, and preliminary vegetative response are discussed in Jones et al. (2005).

Methods

Location.—The ARD and ELRD occur in portions of Tehama, Butte, Plumas, and Lassen counties in the extreme northern Sierra Nevada and southern Cascade mountains of northeastern California in the vicinity of Lassen Peak.

Monitoring.—Our adaptive management-based monitoring strategy in both pine-oak and aspen habitats is designed to investigate the effects of treatment on the following population parameters: total bird abundance, species richness, and the abundance of individual species, with emphasis on a select set of focal species (Table 1). Additionally, by collecting associated vegetation data we can determine the factors influencing these metrics at pre-treatment sites and correlate observed differences to changes in habitat conditions following treatment.

Site Selection and Point Count Protocol.— In the pine-oak project area we established 149 point counts with 73 in stands slated for treatment and 76 in adjacent reference stands. Aspen site-selection involved choosing stands that represented the range of conditions in which aspen are found throughout ELRD. We limited selection to sites that possessed enough aspen to support at least five point count stations spaced 200 m apart. A total of 84 aspen points were established: 15 in areas already treated and the remaining 69 in areas slated for treatment between 2005 and 2012. Since aspen treatments had been occurring since 1996, we attempted to maximize our sample of post-treatment sites in order to provide immediate information on bird response five to seven years post treatment. At both aspen

Table 1. Aspen and pine-oak focal species.

Aspen	Pine-Oak
Red-breasted Sapsuckers	Band-tailed Pigeons
Hairy Woodpeckers	Woodpeckers (All species)
Olive-sided Flycatchers[1]	Warbling Vireos[2]
Western Wood-Pewees	Cassin's Vireos
Dusky Flycatchers	Red-breasted Nuthatches[1]
Warbling Vireos[2]	Western Tanagers[1]
Tree Swallows[2]	Nashville Warblers
Mountain Bluebirds	Black-throated Gray Warblers[1]
Swainson's Thrushes[2]	Hermit Warblers
Oregon Juncos[1]	MacGillivray's Warblers[1]
Chipping Sparrows	Dark-eyed Juncos[1]
MacGillivray's Warblers[1]	Fox Sparrows[1]

[1] California Partners in Flight Coniferous Forest Bird Conservation Plan Focal Species (California Partners in Flight 2002a).

[2] California Partners in Flight Riparian Bird Conservation Plan Focal Species (Riparian Habitat Joint Venture 2004).

and pine-oak projects we conducted standardized five minute multiple distance band point count censuses (Ralph et al. 1993, Buckland et al. 1993).

Focal Species.—Though we are interested in the response of the entire avian community to treatment (e.g., species richness and total bird abundance), focusing on the habitat associations and changes in the relative abundance of individual species is likely to provide more insight to help guide and evaluate management (Burnett et al. 2005). Thus, our analysis for both aspen and pine-black oak projects focuses on a suite of species that represent the range of habitat conditions that we believe would exist under more natural and functional ecological processes.

In selecting focal species we used the basic approach outlined by California Partners in Flight (Chase and Geupel 2005). In fact, the majority of our focal species are those identified in the Coniferous Forest and Riparian Bird Conservation Plans (California Partners in Flight 2002b, Riparian Habitat Joint Venture 2004). Our pine-oak focal species include those with strong affinities for hardwoods such as Warbling Vireos (*Vireo gilvus*), Nashville (*Vermivora ruficapilla*), and Black-throated Gray (*Dendroica nigrescens*) warblers, species of management concern such as woodpeckers and Olive-sided Flycatchers (*Contopus cooperi*), and species that are associated with understory habitat structure such as MacGillivray's Warblers (*Oporornis tolmiei*) and Fox Sparrows (*Passerella iliaca*).

As with our pine-oak project, aspen focal species include those of management interest such as Hairy

Woodpeckers (*Picoides villosus*), those with strong affinities for aspen such as Dusky Flycatchers (*Empidonax oberholseri*) and Warbling Vireos, and those that meet both criteria such as Red-breasted Sapsuckers (*Sphyrapicus ruber*). We also included species associated with early successional/open forest conditions that may be negatively affected by accelerated conifer encroachment in a fire suppression/late seral stage dominated management strategy such as Olive-sided Flycatchers, Mountain Bluebirds (*Sialia currucoides*), and Chipping Sparrows (*Spizella passerina*). Additionally, we are interested in the European Starlings (*Sturnus vulgaris*) and Brown-headed Cowbirds (*Molothrus ater*), two species that may negatively affect avian communities and are often associated with fragmentation and open habitat conditions (see Table 1 for a complete list of aspen and pine-oak focal species).

Complementing the avian monitoring, the Lassen National Forest is conducting vegetation monitoring for both the pine-oak and aspen projects to determine whether the vegetation management objectives are being met (Jones et al. 2005, Tate 2005).

Results

Pine-Oak.—Two years of pre-treatment avian monitoring has revealed that per point indices of species richness and total bird abundance are very similar between our reference and treatment plots. Compared to mixed conifer black oak forest in the adjacent Plumas National Forest the project area had significantly lower avian richness and total bird abundance (Fig. 1). The lower overall richness and abundance suggests the habitat is not simply

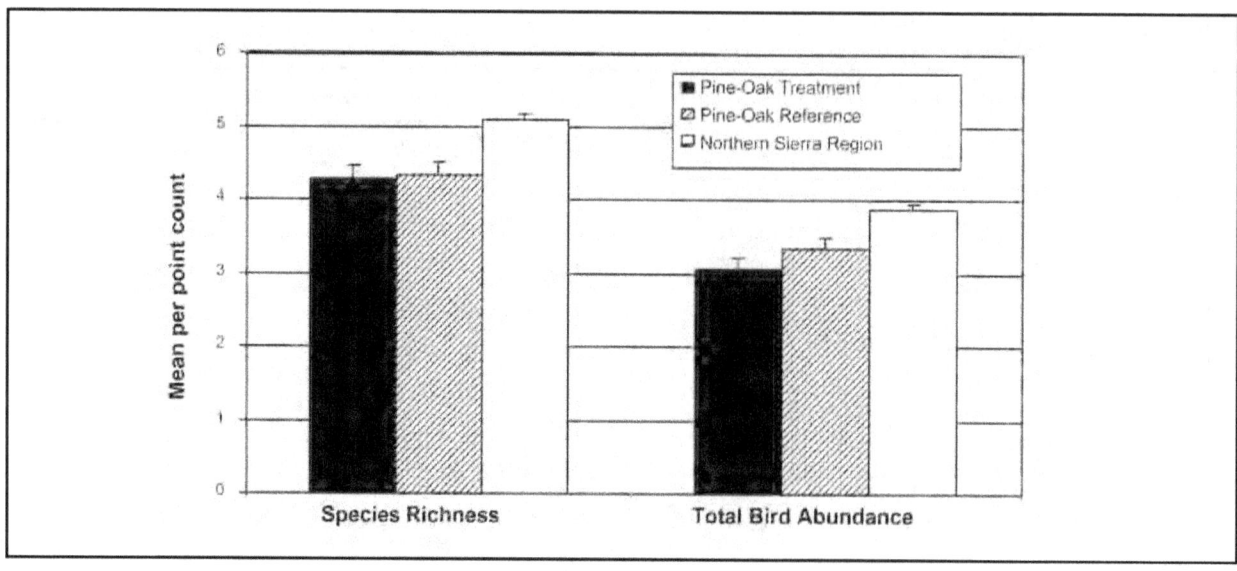

Figure 1. Mean per point per visit species richness and total bird abundance (2004 - 2005) at sites slated for treatment and adjacent reference sites compared to other point count locations in the Northern Sierra where pine-oak is present (+ standard error).

supporting a different suite of species but the encroachment of conifers and apparent reduction in structural diversity has resulted in lower quality avian habitat.

Treatment of the pine-oak project was implemented in 2005 in one-third of the units with the remaining areas scheduled to be treated in 2006 and 2007. We collected our first year of post-treatment data in 2006 and will begin to examine the response of our focal species and the rest of the avian community in the coming years.

Aspen.—The aspen monitoring project began in 2004. Vegetation monitoring by the Lassen National Forest has shown that aspen treatments which remove the majority of encroaching conifers result in a significant increase in aspen cover within the first five years post-treatment (Jones et al. 2005). We were concerned that this approach would negatively affect avian species richness after the removal of the majority of conifers. However, initial avian monitoring has shown that 1 – 8 years post-treatment stands support equal or greater bird species richness and total abundance than untreated stands. Red-breasted Sapsuckers and Hairy Woodpeckers were significantly more abundant in treated aspen sites than at either untreated aspen sites or non-aspen sites (Fig. 2). In total eight species were significantly more abundant in recently treated aspen (< 8 years post treatment) sites (e.g., Mountain Bluebirds, Chipping Sparrows) while only one species (Warbling Vireos) was significantly more abundant in untreated aspen sites.

Our results highlight the importance of an understory aspen component. The number of aspen stems between 0.5 m and 1.4 m tall was the single best predictor of avian species richness in aspen habitat ($R^2 = 0.11$) and was significantly correlated

with the total abundance of cavity nesting species. Also, a number of the most common breeding species in aspen are open-cup understory nesters, such as Dusky Flycatchers, MacGillivray's Warblers, and Chipping Sparrows.

Discussion

Implementing land management techniques that enhance bird conservation on public lands will involve applying the best bird science to inform land management decisions. For 10 years PRBO has worked in partnership with Lassen National Forest to measure the response of birds to management prescriptions, and integrate those results into project planning. The effectiveness of that partnership can be seen in the results of this study, in which we measured the response of the bird community to management prescriptions that enhance pine-oak and aspen habitat.

Pine-Oak.—Although we had not yet conducted monitoring of the specific sites selected for treatment of the pine-oak project, we were still able to provide specific pre-project design recommendations using the approach outlined in Burnett et al. (2005). We used the results from habitat association analysis from our earlier monitoring work and gleaned information from the literature including California Partners in Flight Sierra Nevada and Coniferous Forest Bird Conservation Plans (Siegel and DeSante 1999, California Partners in Flight 2002b). We then synthesized this information along with our knowledge of the avian community to provide a scientifically-based ecological approach for avian habitat enhancement in these vegetation communities.

ARD and ELRD are both planning second generation pine-oak projects that are incorporating

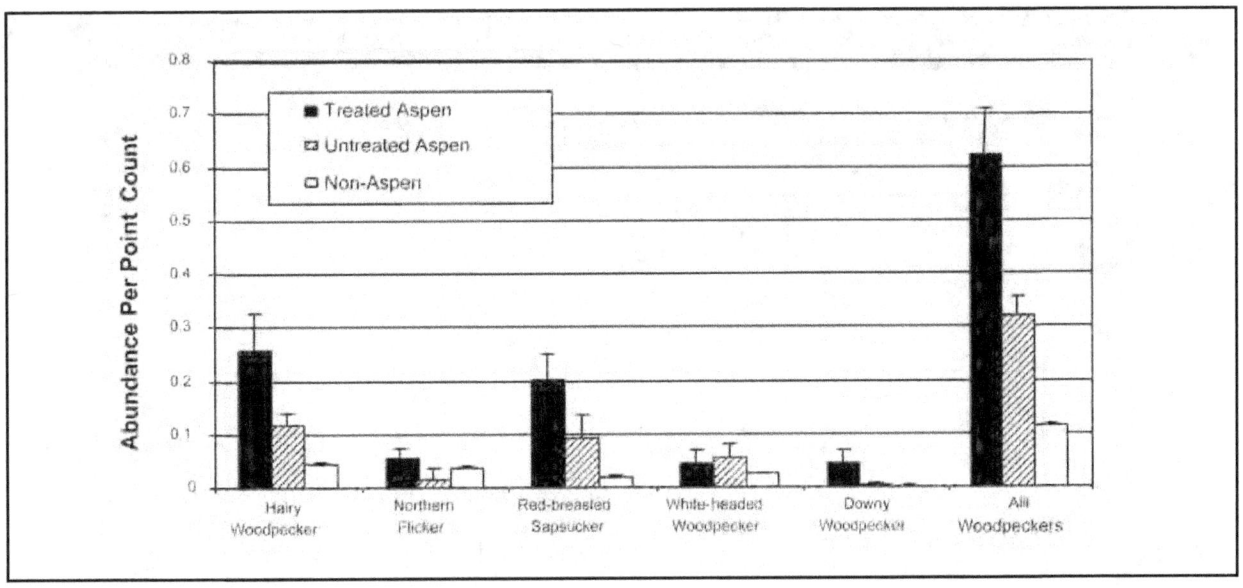

Figure 2. Mean relative abundance per visit (+ standard error) of four woodpecker species detected within 50 m of observers at treated and untreated aspen sites and in non-aspen conifer habitat in the region from 2004 – 2006.

avian and vegetation monitoring results. Following our recommendations, ARD and ELRD have placed a higher priority on retaining snags, creating habitat mosaics, and enhancing shrub and oak growing conditions. They are also planning multiple prescribed burns to increase understory plant vigor and regeneration.

Aspen.—ELRD is using our data to support their aspen approach and to treat more land, including a number of aspen stands associated with riparian areas. ARD is now working to identify and treat aspen habitat following the model of ELRD using our results that show a positive response to treatments as support for such projects. We will be working with both districts using our results from ELRD to provide input into aspen treatments to ensure they maximize benefits to the avian community.

Potentially more important than the adaptive management resulting from our studies is the added commitment from the Lassen National Forest to include monitoring of new pine-oak and aspen enhancement projects. In 2006, we began monitoring ARD's first major aspen enhancement project, which will treat over 80 ha of degraded and encroached aspen.

Our results have helped secure funding and prioritization of aspen enhancement on ARD, and ELRD is now planning a project to enhance pine-oak habitat. We will be working with the Lassen National Forest to incorporate what we have learned from monitoring these pilot projects into the second generation of pine-oak and aspen enhancement projects being planned now. We have also received interest from the Plumas National forest on using our results to help guide their future aspen and pine-oak projects.

While we feel we have played an important role in habitat enhancement projects occurring on the Lassen National Forest, our partners, especially the biologists and district rangers, deserve most of the credit for having the foresight to pursue these projects, fund monitoring, and support an adaptive management approach. By working at the ranger district level, it is possible to integrate results-driven recommendations into forest management and encourage an environment of adaptive management. Working with the local district personnel on these projects allows us to provide highly relevant data pertinent for adapting old strategies to improve habitat for birds and other wildlife. We continue to work with the district staff to find the most appropriate and efficient avenues for using our results to help guide future management and ensure these projects have the greatest possible benefit to the avian community.

Acknowledgments

I thank the U.S. Forest Service staff that had the foresight to support adaptive management and habitat enhancement. Specifically, I thank Tom H. Rickman, Bobette E. Jones, and Bob Andrews of the ELRD and Mark R. Williams, Coye L. Burnett, Alfred G. Vasquez of the ARD. I also thank the numerous dedicated field biologists who worked so hard collecting data. Diana Humple and three anonymous reviewers provided valuable feedback to help improve an earlier version of this paper. PRBO's Northern Sierra program is funded by the Lassen National Forest, Region 5 of the USFS, and the National Fire Plan. This is PRBO contribution 1516.

Partial Harvesting Can Enhance Foraging Habitat for Birds Associated with Understory Vegetation in Western Oregon Forests

Joan C. Hagar

Abstract

Forest management activities can influence arthropods that dwell in the understory by affecting the structure and composition of understory vegetation. Changes in abundance and species composition of arthropod communities in turn may influence the distribution and abundance of avian insectivores. I examined the relationship between bird abundance and occurrence, and cover of understory plant species that have been identified as being important in supporting arthropod prey. I compared bird abundance and shrub cover among silvicultural treatments in managed and unmanaged Douglas-fir (*Pseudotsuga menziesii*) forests in western Oregon. Greater cover of oceanspray (*Holodiscus discolor*), California hazel (*Corylus cornuta*), and bracken fern (*Pteridium aquilinum*) in stands where canopy had been reduced corresponded to higher abundances of three shrub-associated bird species. Stands occupied by Wilson's (*Wilsonia pusilla*) and MacGillivray's (*Oporornis tomiei*) warblers had greater cover of deciduous shrubs than unoccupied stands. Shrub species that make an important contribution to food resources for birds in conifer-dominated habitats can be enhanced through management of the density of overstory trees.

Introduction

The maintenance of biodiversity in young, managed forests is an objective for many forest managers, and is legally mandated on federal forest lands (U.S. Department of Agriculture and U.S. Department of the Interior 1994b). Goals of the Northwest Forest Plan include promoting biodiversity in both designated reserves and in stands managed for timber production. Young (< 100 years) forests currently occupy much of the land under the jurisdiction of the Northwest Forest Plan. Young stands that are the legacy of past clear-cut harvesting often lack the structural heterogeneity of natural stands (Hansen et al. 1991). One important structural feature that is typically not well developed in dense young stands is understory vegetation. Management techniques that promote early and sustained conifer dominance in managed forests, such as planting high densities of tree seedlings at stand initiation, shorten the period of herb and shrub dominance following harvest and reduce the abundance and distribution of understory vegetation and hardwoods in developing stands through shading (Hansen et al. 1991). Shrubby understories in young forests and/or early seral shrub fields are a primary breeding habitat for several species of songbirds, including Swainson's Thrushes (*Catharus ustulatus*), Wilson's (*Wilsonia pusilla*), MacGillivray's (*Oporornis tolmiei*), and Orange-crowned (*Vermivora celata*) warblers (Dillingham 2003; Dowlan 2003; Hagar 2003a, 2003b). Populations of these four species have decreased in all or portions of their western North America breeding range over the past three decades (Sauer et al. 2005). Managers concerned with the maintenance of biodiversity have a critical need for information and tools that will allow them to provide habitat for species with declining populations.

Partial harvests such as thinning and group selection are among the practices being developed to simultaneously manage forests for biodiversity and timber production (McComb et al. 1993, Chambers 1996, Carey et al. 1999). Thinning is an intermediate harvest in an even-aged management system (i.e., implemented between stand establishment and final clear-cut harvest) that reduces stand density by removing selected stems according to criteria based on spacing, diameter, or dominance of residual trees. Group selection removes small groups of trees in uneven-aged management systems, typically creating gaps of about 0.1 to 0.2 ha (0.25 to 0.5 ac) in size. These practices have the potential to increase structural diversity by increasing the availability of light and other resources for vegetation below the forest canopy. It may be possible to use canopy removal to promote particular species of understory shrubs that provide valuable habitat for birds. For example, oceanspray (*Holodiscus discolor*), California hazel (*Corylus cornuta*), and bracken fern (*Pteridium aquilinum*) support a relatively high abundance and biomass of arthropod prey for insectivorous birds (Hammond and Miller 1998, Doolittle 2000, Hagar et al. 2007). Oceanspray may be particularly important in supporting prey for birds because it supports both a high diversity and a high abundance of Lepidoptera (Hammond and Miller 1998, Muir et al. 2002), a favored food of many insectivorous birds (Graber and Graber 1983, Holmes 1990). Although oceanspray and California hazel frequently occur under closed canopy, they can achieve greater cover and density under incomplete canopy and generally respond positively to a reduction of overstory cover (Thomas et al. 1999, Thysell and Carey 2000). Bracken fern also can become abundant following disturbances such as thinning (Crane 1990). However, partial harvests traditionally have been used for timber production and their use as tools for managing wildlife habitat needs to be refined. Managers need more information on the responses of birds and shrubs to silvicultural manipulations of stand structure to help them provide quality habitats through modified thinning prescriptions. In this study, I examined the relationship between bird abundance and occurrence, cover of selected understory plants, and silvicultural treatment.

Methods

Project Description.—This study was initiated as part of a larger project that addressed the need to understand the contribution of thinning as a management tool for fostering biodiversity in western Oregon forests (Muir et al. 2002). The goal of this integrated effort was to develop tools and indicators for maintaining and monitoring biodiversity in young conifer forests. The goal of my study was to identify plant species that may be important in supporting food resources for songbirds associated with understories in Pacific Northwest conifer forests, and to assess the influence of partial overstory removal on these resources.

This project was located in the central Oregon Coast Range, in the western hemlock (*Tsuga heterophylla*) forest zone (Franklin and Dyrness 1988). Sites were located on public lands managed by three agencies: Siuslaw National Forest, Salem District of the Bureau of Land Management, and Oregon State University. Other partners involved in the project included USGS-Forest and Rangeland Ecosystem Science Center, and the Cooperative Forest Ecosystem Research program.

Management Goals.—The questions of interest in my study were:
(1) Does abundance of four shrub-dwelling bird species differ among silvicultural treatments?;

(2) How does partial removal of the overstory influence the cover of plant species that support the most arthropod prey?;

(3) Is stand level habitat occupancy associated with cover of deciduous shrubs?

To address these questions I compared bird abundance and shrub cover between stands that had been thinned or harvested with group selection and their unharvested counterparts. Thinning had been performed 15 to 20 years prior to the study

in young (approximately 50 years old) stands using traditional methods that favored the development of conifers with large stems and crowns, minimized canopy openings, and produced regular spacing among residual stems. Although these stands had been thinned with the goal of optimizing timber production, the intensity of thinning had in some cases been sufficient to promote development of understory vegetation. Thus, thinned young stands represented a potential treatment for increasing structural and biological diversity in young forests, and were compared to young unthinned stands that represented a forest condition currently dominating many Pacific Northwest landscapes. In addition, I compared older stands with and without partial harvesting. Older stands, approximately 120 years old, that had been partially harvested nine years prior to this study with group selection represented an alternative regeneration method to clear-cut harvesting that may offer options for maintaining habitat for understory species in older stands (McComb et al. 1993). I compared group selection stands to unharvested stands of a similar age (hereafter referred to as "mature" stands).

Monitoring Regime.—I conducted point counts of breeding birds (Reynolds et al. 1980) to estimate abundance and occurrence of each species on the study sites and to compare among silvicultural treatments. I focused these comparisons on Swainson's Thrushes, Wilson's, MacGillivray's, and Orange-crowned warblers because these species forage extensively in the understory (Marshall et al. 2003). Vegetation cover was estimated using line transects (Brower et al.1990) and compared among silvicultural treatments.

Results

Bracken fern, oceanspray, and California hazel support high biomass of arthropod prey relative to other understory species in the Oregon Coast Ranges (Doolittle 2000, Hagar et al. 2007). These deciduous species can achieve greater cover and density under incomplete canopy (Thomas et al. 1999, Thysell and Carey 2000). In western Oregon, cover of bracken fern is more extensive in thinned stands than in unthinned and mature stands, where cover is typically low or negligible (Bailey et al. 1998, Crane 1990, Doolittle 2000, Muir et al. 2002). This also was true on my study sites, where bracken fern cover was greater in stands that had been partially harvested than in similar stands that had not been harvested (Fig. 1). In addition, although differences were not statistically significant, oceanspray cover tended to be greater in thinned than unthinned stands, and California hazel cover tended to be greater in group selection compared to unharvested mature stands (Fig. 1).

Partially harvested stands supported greater abundances of the four shrub-associated birds studied than unharvested stands. Wilson's Warblers were observed in all stands, but median abundance was more than six times greater in group selection

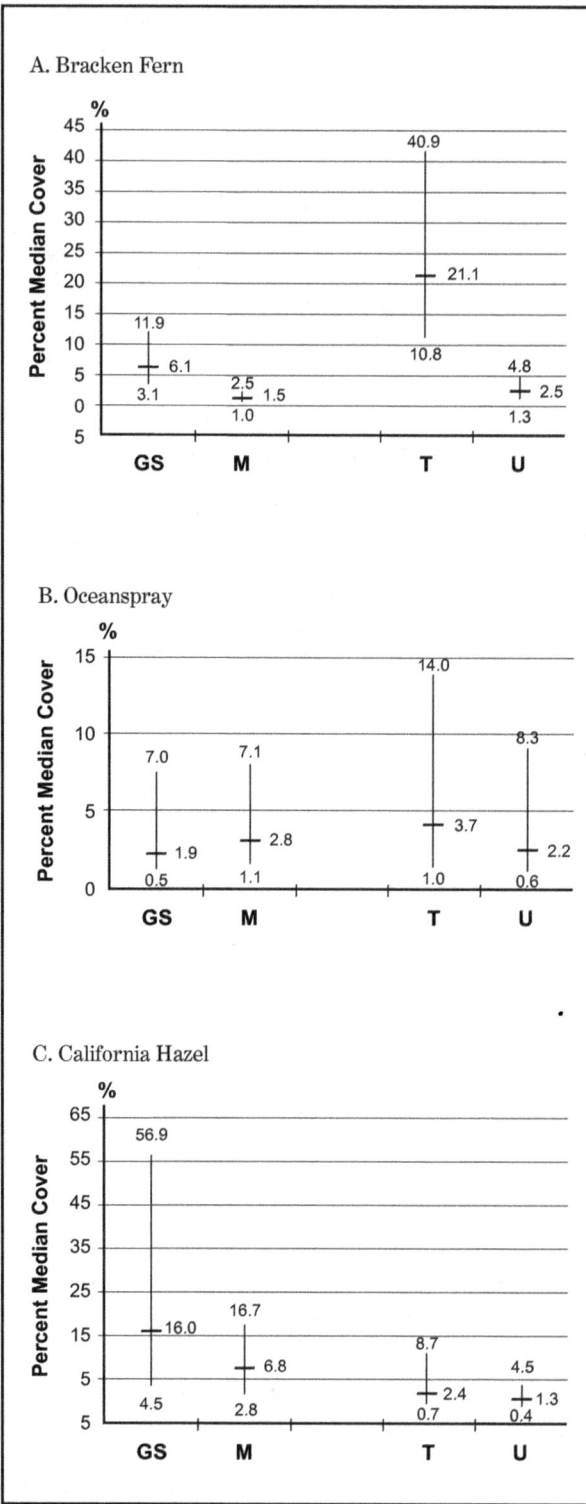

Figure 1. Median cover with 90% confidence intervals for bracken fern, oceanspray, and California hazel, (within 2 m of forest floor) in two types of partial harvest (GS: group selection and T: young thinned), and two unharvested types (M: mature and U: young unthinned) in the Oregon Coast Range, 1999.

and thinned conditions than in mature and unthinned (Fig. 2A). Average abundance of MacGillivray's Warblers in group selection stands was more than ten times greater than in mature and almost four times greater than in unthinned stands (Fig. 2B). Eighty-six percent of the observations of Orange-crowned Warblers were in group selection stands; they rarely were observed in mature, thinned, and unthinned stands (Fig. 2C). Average abundance of Swainson's Thrushes was greater in group selection than unharvested mature stands, but greater average abundance in thinned than unthinned stands was not statistically significant (Fig. 2D). For Wilson's and MacGillivray's warblers, percent cover of deciduous vegetation in the understory was an important factor in stand-level selection of habitat; both species were less commonly detected in stands that averaged less than 35% cover of deciduous shrubs (Fig. 3). Greater arthropod prey biomass on deciduous species such as bracken fern and oceanspray may have influenced selection of this habitat by birds (Hagar et al. 2007). Swainson's Thrushes occurred in all stands surveyed, so a comparison of deciduous cover between occupied and unoccupied stands was not possible. My results provide support for the hypothesis that partial removal of overstory in dense stands may improve habitat for shrub-associated bird species by promoting the development of understory vegetation that supports arthropod prey.

Discussion

Implications for Management.—The application of partial harvesting to enhance diversity is relatively recent, mostly having been implemented within the last decade. Bird monitoring results indicate that the benefits to shrub-associated bird species are conditional on the impact of harvest and the time required for recovery of understory shrubs. The mechanical process of thinning may damage tall shrubs, resulting in a short-term decrease of shrub cover (Curtis et al. 1998) and a corresponding decrease in habitat suitability for species associated with tall shrubs. Furthermore, differences in abundance of understory plants between thinned and unthinned stands in the Coast Range may take more than a decade to emerge (Alaback and Herman 1988). A positive response of Swainson's Thrushes and Wilson's Warblers to partial overstory removal may be delayed until a dense layer of tall shrubs develops.

These results suggest that silvicultural prescriptions that explicitly address goals for structure and composition of shrubs may be a strategy for increasing functional as well as structural diversity in managed stands. Modifications to conventional thinning, including wider spacing, uneven spacing, and protection of shrubs during harvest operations may be required to achieve desired shrub cover. Commercial thinning implemented at a sufficiently heavy intensity can favor the establishment and expansion of many shrub species, leading to the

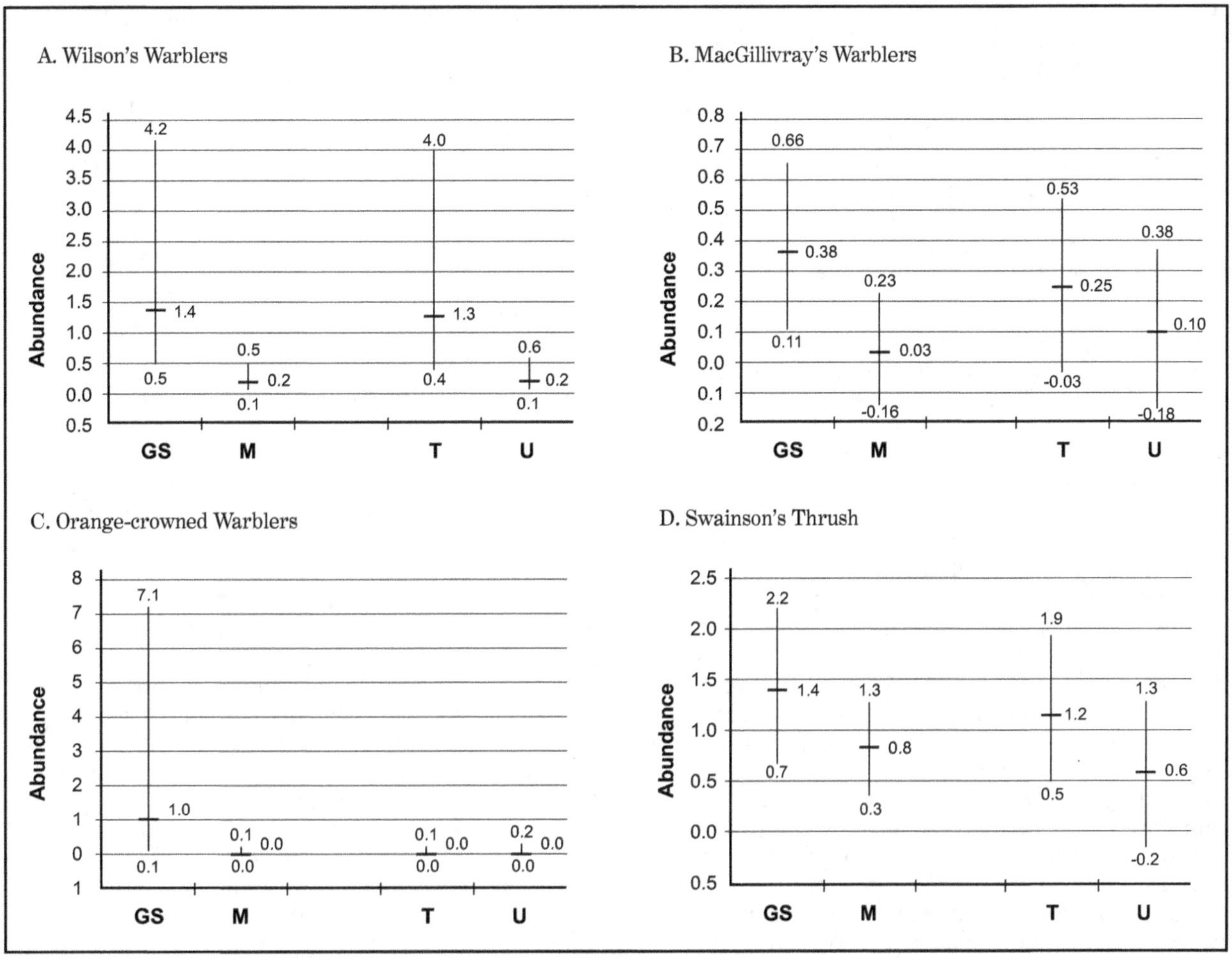

A. Wilson's Warblers

B. MacGillivray's Warblers

C. Orange-crowned Warblers

D. Swainson's Thrush

Figure 2. Median (Wilson's and Orange-crowned warblers) or mean (Swainson's Thrushes and MacGillivray's Warblers) abundance index (birds/stand/visit) with 90% confidence intervals in two types of partial harvest (GS: group selection and T: young thinned), and two unharvested types (M: mature and U: young unthinned) in the Oregon Coast Range, 1999.

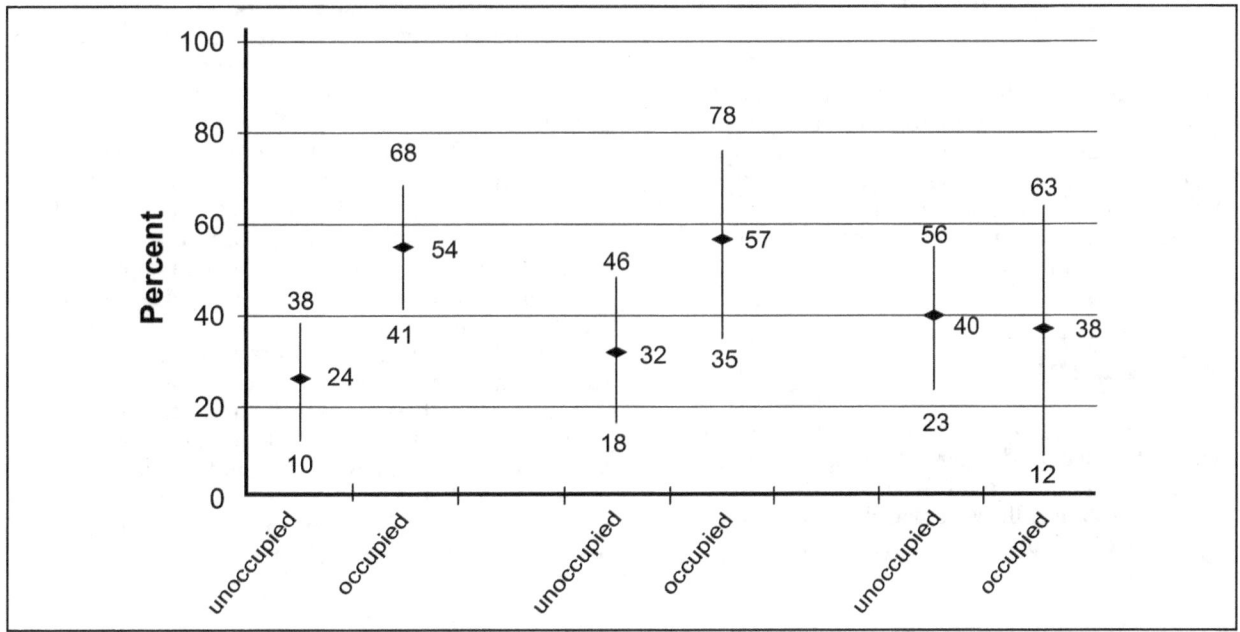

Figure 3. Average percent cover (with 90% CI) of deciduous shrubs (y-axis) in Oregon Coast Range Douglas-fir stands where selected bird species were detected (occupied) and were not detected (unoccupied) during breeding season, 1999.

development of a vigorous understory (Tappeiner and Zasada 1993, Huffman et al. 1994). In forests managed under long rotations or an uneven-aged system, group selection or other partial harvests may help maintain understory vegetation by creating gaps in the forest canopy. Allowing the development of shrubs that support arthropod prey in at least some of these gaps, rather than managing intensively for the next cohort of conifer trees, may be one strategy for promoting habitat for songbirds.

Monitoring the Effectiveness of Forest Treatments.—In general, partial harvests have the potential to significantly increase habitat availability for shrub-associated birds over unthinned plantations, but continued monitoring will be necessary to assess long-term impacts. An ultimate goal of this work is to facilitate management for biodiversity by considering the habitat requirements of multiple species simultaneously. My approach indirectly links three important components of biodiversity in Pacific Northwest forest ecosystems: understory vegetation, arthropods, and songbirds. Ideally, once these relationships are well established, monitoring focused on one group (shrubs, arthropods, or birds) may provide important information about the status of resource availability for the other components. Birds can be monitored with standard point count methodology (Ralph et al. 1995) to document abundance and species composition, and to confirm presence of desired species. Monitoring of understory vegetation in stands managed for Wilson's and MacGillivray's warblers can be implemented to ensure that at least 35% cover of deciduous shrubs is maintained. Information on demographics, survival, and reproductive output would provide the best indication of habitat value for these birds, and could be obtained through constant-effort mist-netting (Dunn and Ralph 2004).

It may be desirable, but probably not logistically feasible for most managers, to monitor arthropods. However, if resources are available for arthropod monitoring, caterpillars would be a good group on which to focus because of their importance as prey and because they can easily be sampled by the vegetation beating method.

Conclusion

The positive associations among cover of deciduous shrubs, abundance of foliage-dwelling arthropod prey, and the abundance of Swainson's Thrushes, Wilson's and MacGillivray's warblers suggest that the presence and amount of deciduous vegetation

in the forest understory are important habitat components for these bird species (Whitaker et al. 2000, Brush and Stiles 1986). My findings support the use of partial harvesting as a tool for maintaining deciduous shrubs in managed forests in order to provide habitat for some species of insectivorous birds.

It is clear that even conventionally implemented thinning has the potential to increase habitat availability for shrub-associated birds over unthinned plantations, as does group selection harvesting. Managers who want to further adapt these tools for promoting bird habitat could experiment with a range of thinning intensities and patterns, and monitor responses of shrubs and shrub-associated bird species. For example, variable density thinning has been recommended as a strategy for promoting understory development and structural diversity in managed conifer stands (Carey et al. 1999). Constraints such as economic goals, stand susceptibility to windthrow, and goals related to other resources may be factors in determining the range of thinning options feasible for each land owner. Management of density with pre-commercial and commercial thinning starting early in stand development may be a good strategy for retaining continuous cover of desired understory vegetation over time, throughout the life of a forest stand (Tappeiner et al.2002). This strategy may create conditions more similar to natural regeneration following a stand-replacing natural disturbance, such as a fire. Enhancing structure with thinning may be unnecessary in stands that develop with sufficient shrub cover and retain it through mid- seral stages.

Several studies have demonstrated that species richness of songbird assemblages increases in response to thinning of dense conifer stands that have developed under a clear-cut regeneration system in moist Pacific Northwest forests (Hagar et al. 1996, Hayes et al. 1997, Haveri and Carey 2000, Hayes et al. 2003, Hagar et al. 2004). However, some species may be negatively affected by thinning. The abundance of some species that are associated with dense conifer canopies is often reduced in thinned stands in the short-term. A reasonable approach to providing suitable habitat for these species would be to retain conifer stands with dense, closed canopies at various spatial scales on forested landscapes. Thinning also can result in reduced production of coarse woody debris, a critically important habitat component for many species of wildlife (Rose et al. 2001). Managers who want to maintain habitat for a diversity of forest wildlife can include plans for recruitment of woody debris in prescriptions that employ thinning for diversity.

Success in Recovery Efforts of the Least Bell's Vireo in Southern California

Barbara E. Kus

Abstract

Least Bell's Vireos (*Vireo bellii pusillus*) are migratory riparian obligates that two decades ago were on the brink of extinction as a result of habitat loss and degradation, and secondarily, Brown-headed Cowbird (*Molothrus ater*) parasitism, throughout their California range. Management to arrest and reverse declines in the remaining populations has focused on cowbird control and habitat restoration. Annual trapping and removal of Brown-headed Cowbirds from Least Bell's Vireo breeding sites has reduced or eliminated parasitism and resulted in a doubling or tripling of seasonal production of young relative to pre-trapping years. Habitat created through the planting of young shrubs and trees can attain the structural features of natural riparian habitat within 3-5 years, and provide foraging and nesting sites for Least Bell's Vireos. As a result of these recovery efforts, the Least Bell's Vireo population is ten times larger than in 1986 when it was listed as Endangered under the Endangered Species Act. Continued population growth and range expansion through these and other means will rely on cooperation and creative partnerships among multiple stakeholders to design, fund, implement, and monitor management efforts for Least Bell's Vireos and other riparian inhabitants.

Introduction

Least Bell's Vireos (*Vireo bellii pusillus*) are small, migratory songbirds dependent on riparian habitat for breeding. Early naturalists described the species as a common inhabitant of lowland riparian areas throughout California (Grinnell and Miller 1944), but by the second half of the twentieth century, Least Bell's Vireo numbers were plummeting as expanding human activities in floodplains destroyed or degraded over 90% of the state's riparian habitat. Although many riparian bird species declined during this same period, Least Bell's Vireos were particularly affected because of their high vulnerability to parasitism by Brown-headed Cowbirds (*Molothrus ater*), which expanded rapidly from the lower Colorado River west and north into California during the early 1900's (Laymon 1987). Parasitism is believed to have further reduced already small and fragmented populations and accelerated declines. By 1986, when the species was listed as federally endangered, vireos had been extirpated from most of their historic range, and numbered just 300 territorial males occupying a handful of southern California drainages (U.S. Fish and Wildlife Service 1998). Viewed as the first of potentially many other species facing similar fates, Least Bell's Vireos are considered a flagship species within the context of riparian habitat conservation, and serves as a focal point for management to protect riparian communities in general.

Management for the Least Bell's Vireos (vireo) has been directed toward two goals: eliminating or reducing cowbird parasitism in remaining populations, and increasing the availability of suitable breeding habitat. These efforts have been pursued through the coordinated actions of numerous federal, state, local, and non-governmental organizations including the U.S. Fish and Wildlife Service, U.S. Marine Corps, U.S. Army Corps of Engineers, International Boundary and Water Commission, California Department of Fish and Game, California Department of Transportation, and California Department of Parks and Recreation.

Controlling Parasitism

Brown-headed Cowbirds (cowbird) occur in every drainage occupied by vireos in southern California, where they are attracted by the high concentration of hosts in the riparian habitat and the foraging opportunities provided by nearby dairies, equestrian centers, golf courses, agricultural fields, pastures, and residential areas. Efforts to control parasitism began soon after vireos were listed, and rapidly became a standard component of mitigation requirements for development projects affecting vireo habitat. Cowbirds are removed annually from riparian areas using modified Australian Crow traps baited with seed and live decoy birds (Griffith and Griffith 2000), under a permit from the U.S. Fish and Wildlife Service. At some sites, vireo nests are monitored to detect and remove (or addle) any cowbird eggs. When combined with trapping, nest monitoring provides an additional layer of protection against parasitism, and yields the data necessary for evaluating the effectiveness of cowbird control measures.

Several sites in San Diego County have now been managed and monitored consistently for nearly two decades, including Marine Corps Base Camp Pendleton, the San Luis Rey River, and the San Diego River. Not only are long-term data available on parasitism rates, nest success, and population growth under cowbird management (Griffith and Griffith 2000, Kus and Whitfield 2005), but data before the implementation of cowbird control exist for these sites, allowing a rare perspective on the response of vireos to management. Analysis of the relationship between annual parasitism rate (the proportion of nests parasitized), which ranged from 0-80% across the three sites, and the number of vireo young fledged per pair over the course of the season, showed that parasitism is a major determinant of productivity, accounting for 65% of the annual variability in production of young (Kus and Whitfield 2005). These findings quantify the magnitude of the effect of parasitism on productivity, and indicate that management of cowbirds is targeting a primary factor limiting vireo population growth. Moreover, the data incorporate a broad range of geographical and annual climatic (e.g., precipitation) conditions under which vireo populations exist, suggesting that the relationship is robust to variable spatial and temporal influences.

Implementation of cowbird control significantly reduced parasitism relative to pre-trapping years at all three sites (Kus and Whitfield 2005; Table 1). The most extreme decline occurred at Camp Pendleton, where parasitism dropped 10-fold from an average of 47% of nests parasitized during two years preceding trapping to 4% during 15 years after control was initiated. Variability across sites in the extent to which parasitism has been reduced by cowbird control is in part a reflection of the adequacy of trapping relative to the size of the local cowbird population. For example, logistical challenges, including access to private property, have historically constrained the number, operation, and locations of cowbird traps along the San Luis Rey River. Parasitism at this site has typically been higher than at other sites as a result. Nevertheless, even here cowbird trapping has cut the rate of nest parasitism in half relative to the pre-trapping rate (Table 1).

Associated with declines in parasitism have been increases in seasonal production of vireo young, which doubled relative to pre-trapping years at Camp Pendleton and tripled at the San Luis Rey River (Table 1). At the San Diego River, annual productivity increased from under one young per pair to an average of 2.9 young per pair, the highest level of productivity recorded for any Least Bell's Vireo population with long-term monitoring. Notably, annual productivity at all three sites increased to nearly meet or exceed the level estimated necessary for maintenance of stable populations of vireos, two young per female (Franzreb 1989).

While increasing production of young through cowbird control provides a mechanism for managing endangered hosts, the currency of recovery is actual population growth. Nowhere has this growth been more spectacular than at Camp Pendleton, where a population numbering 27 territories in 1981 grew to over 1000 territories in 1998 (Griffith and Griffith 2000, Kus and Whitfield 2005; Fig. 1). Some, but not all, of this population growth over two decades may be attributable to an increase in suitable habitat. Vireo numbers at the San Luis Rey River also increased after cowbird control was initiated, from 24 territories in 1984 to 132 territories in 1999. Increases at the San Diego River have been more modest, with numbers of vireo territories growing from the low 20s to the high 30s during a 13-year period. It is likely that this latter population was approaching carrying capacity at the time cowbird control was initiated, limiting the capacity for further growth. After 15-20 years of growth, even the larger populations at Camp Pendleton and the San Luis Rey River appear to have reached a plateau suggesting that habitat availability is now limiting further growth (Fig. 1). Fluctuations in both of these populations since their peaks in the late 1990's have coincided with periods of record-

Table 1. Percent of nests parasitized, and seasonal productivity of Least Bell's Vireos before and after Brown-headed Cowbird trapping at three sites in San Diego County, California. Numbers in parentheses are number of years. *P* values are for independent sample, one-tailed t-tests. Annual sample sizes (number of nests with eggs): Pendleton: 15-93 (pre-control), 26-244 (post-control); San Diego: 25-40 (pre-control), 29-62 (post-control); San Luis Rey: 11-37 (pre-control), 29-125 (post-control).

Parameter	Site	Pre-control	Post-control	P
Nests Parasitized	Pendleton	47 (2)	4 (15)	< 0.001
	San Diego	57 (2)	11 (10)	0.001
	San Luis Rey	63 (2)	32 (9)	< 0.001
Fledglings per Pair	Pendleton	1.4 (2)	2.7 (15)	0.003
	San Diego	0.9 (2)	2.9 (10)	0.01
	San Luis Rey	0.6 (2)	1.9 (9)	0.002

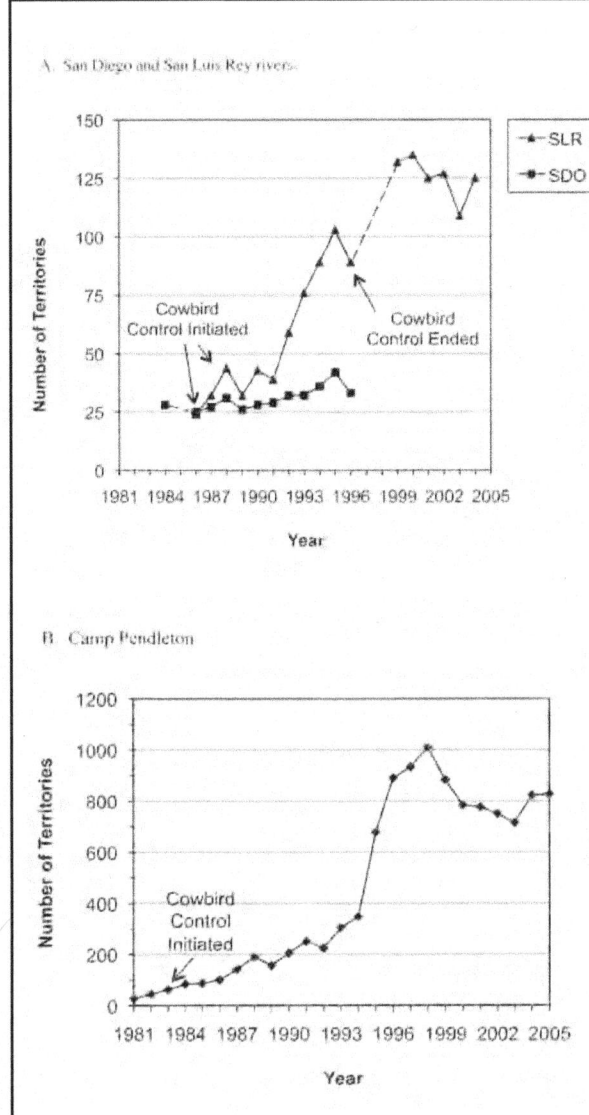

Figure 1. Number of Least Bell's Vireos at A. San Diego (SDO) and San Luis Rey (SLR) Rivers, and B. Camp Pendleton between 1981 and 2005. Note difference in scales between A and B. Dashed lines connect points bracketing years without surveys.

breaking drought, flooding, and at Camp Pendleton, a large scale exotic plant removal program, all of which have reduced availability of suitable nesting habitat.

Habitat Restoration

Providing habitat for vireos, as with cowbird control, has been pursued largely within the context of mitigation for development projects, where habitat creation and restoration are used to avoid a net loss of vireo habitat. Restoration ecology was an emerging and uncertain science in the mid-1980s when creating vireo habitat was first attempted. The design of most restoration projects was driven by a desire for rapid development of habitat because they were linked to short construction timelines.

The standard approach has been to grade sites to within a desired distance of the water table, and plant them with a mix of native trees and shrubs using cuttings, nursery stock, and transplanted mature trees salvaged from the project site (Baird 1989, Baird and Rieger 1989). Sites are weeded and irrigated with drip and/or overhead watering systems until established. Depending on the particular mitigation requirements, most sites are small, generally ranging between 3 and 20 ha in size, yet large enough to support one or more vireo territories.

Vireos use restored sites when these sites achieve structural characteristics typical of vireo nest sites in natural reference habitat (Kus 1998). By sampling planted vegetation annually and comparing it to a habitat suitability model quantifying the vertical distribution of vegetation cover at vireo nest sites, we have seen that restored habitat can attain the structure of model habitat within 3-5 years depending on annual precipitation (Fig. 2). Vireo use of planted sites is associated with the degree of vertical and horizontal development of vegetation. Initially, vireos in nearby habitat visit young sites to forage there, often in family groups that wander beyond the boundaries of their territories after young are fledged. As planted cover increases, vireos adjacent to restored habitat incorporate planted vegetation into their territories, but limit nest placement to the denser vegetation within mature habitat. Not until part or all of a planted site achieves the structural criteria of the suitability model (Fig. 2) do vireos establish territories entirely within created habitat, and place nests there (Kus 1998).

While colonization of planted sites is an encouraging indication that creating vireo habitat is possible, it is necessary that breeding success be comparable in restored and natural sites before the former can be considered effective in providing suitable habitat. This is especially critical within the context of mitigation, where created sites are intended to replace existing functional habitat supporting breeding vireos. We compared seasonal productivity of pairs nesting in created and nearby reference habitat, and while our sample sizes for created sites are small, we found that in most years vireos nesting in restored habitat fledged as many if not more young as did pairs nesting in natural habitat (Kus 1998).

Where Do We Go From Here?

A partnership between research and management during the last two decades has created opportunities to implement and evaluate the effectiveness of various strategies for recovering the vireo. Through this partnership, we have learned that cowbird control has been highly effective as a short-term measure for reversing population declines, and that habitat restoration holds promise as a means of increasing habitat availability. As a

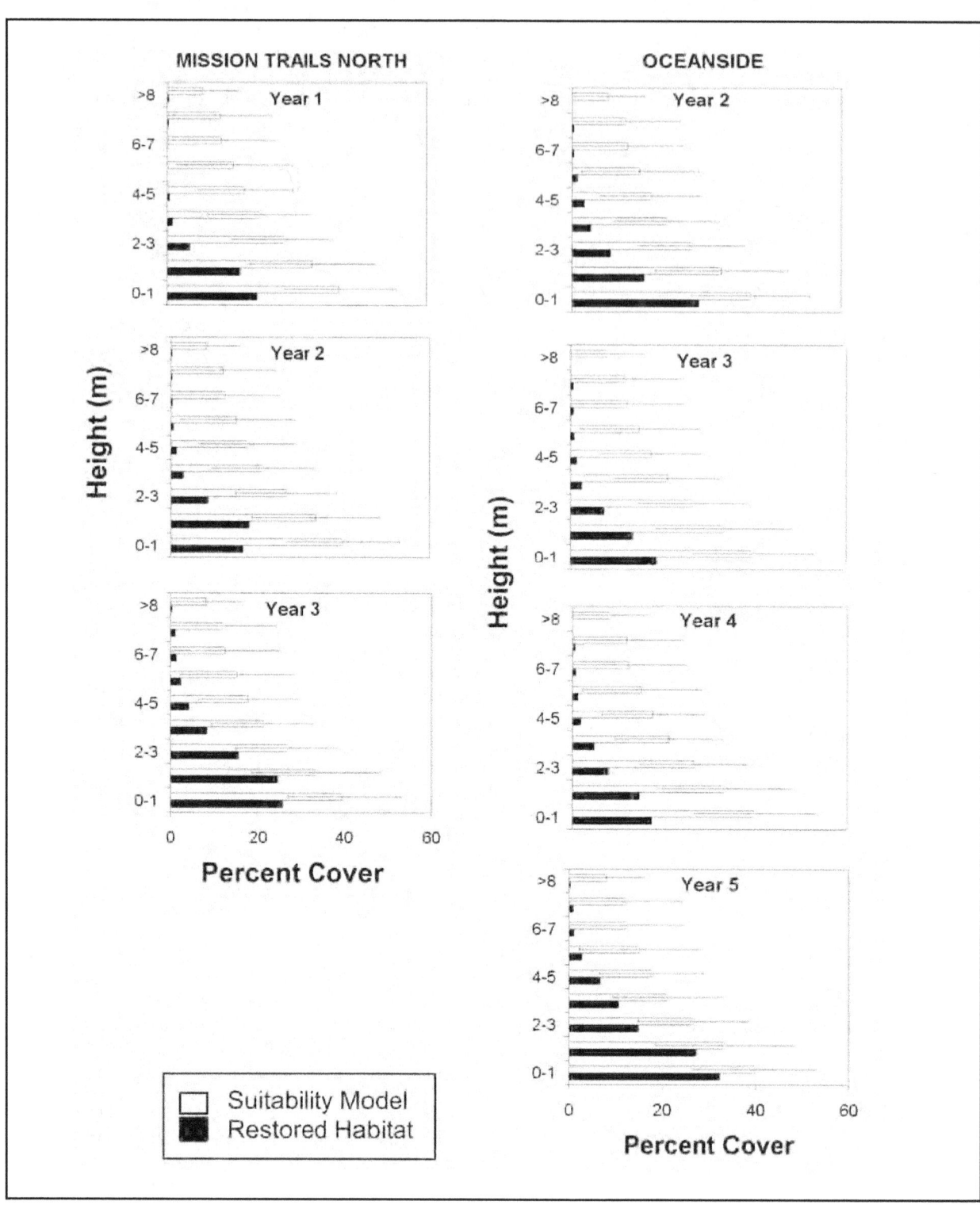

Figure 2. Development of foliage cover at two restored sites relative to vireo habitat suitability model. Model represents means ± 2 SD; bars bracket range of cover defined as suitable nesting habitat. Year 3 at the Mission Trails North site, and Year 5 at the Oceanside site, followed winters of above average precipitation (after Kus 1998).

result, vireos have increased nearly 10-fold since the time of listing, and today number between 2500 and 3000 statewide (B. Kus and L. Hays, pers. comm.). Not only has vireo abundance increased, but distribution as well, expanding northward as birds recolonize their historic range. The exciting discovery of a pair of nesting vireos along the San Joaquin River in 2005 (Kreitinger and Wood 2005) creates anticipation that vireos may once again occupy the Central Valley in the foreseeable future.

We thus find ourselves at an enviable stage of endangered species recovery, where we are able to move beyond crisis management with realistic optimism that the vireo is recoverable. We now have the opportunity to consider ways to refine our tools for recovery so as to maximize the biological effectiveness of our efforts derived from scarce conservation resources, with the ultimate goal of freeing vireos from their dependency on human intervention. How far we move toward this goal will depend on the effective application of knowledge gained through experimentation, in an adaptive management framework.

The primary information need as we enter the next phase of recovery-oriented management is to determine what is required for self-sustaining vireo populations and habitats. With regard to cowbird parasitism, we need to know what level of parasitism can be tolerated by stable populations, and whether this level differs as a function of vireo population size. Sites such as the San Luis Rey River site discussed earlier, where cowbird trapping has been discontinued (Fig. 1), play an invaluable role in addressing these questions by providing a rare opportunity to examine a population's ability to persist in the absence of aggressive cowbird control; studies are currently underway to document this response. Trapping need not cease completely to advance this research, and additional study sites are needed to study vireo response to alternative methods of cowbird control. For example, cowbird trapping intensity could be varied by systematically altering the number of traps, timing of operation, and frequency (annual, bi-annual, etc.) of operation. Information needs relative to habitat creation include comparing alternative planting techniques and continued documentation over time of the capacities of sites for successional change and associated use by vireos. Habitat enhancements that reduce the vulnerability of vireo nests to parasitism, such as dense understory spatially removed from concentrations of tall trees used as cowbird perches (Sharp and Kus 2006), should be pursued and monitored, as should the removal of invasive exotic vegetation as a tool for restoring cover and structural complexity of native riparian habitat. Improving our knowledge of habitat creation and enhancement will depend on an analysis of both the failures and successes of past habitat creation efforts.

Continued progress towards vireo recovery will rely not only on an increased understanding of the biological needs of this species, but also on our ability to apply this knowledge effectively in partnership with many different types of land owners. Vireos occupy a landscape that is owned, managed, and regulated by a large and diverse group of private and public individuals, agencies, and other entities, which complicates the implementation of management actions, such as cowbird control and exotic plant removal, that depend on cooperation and coordination among "stakeholders" for their success. Indeed, the earliest and greatest successes in vireo recovery thus far have come from populations occupying large expanses of land under the management of one or a small number of managers, such as Department of Defense at Camp Pendleton. At the other extreme is the Santa Clara River in Ventura County, where inadequate funding and coordination among the multiple landowners along the river's 50 km length have plagued efforts to manage and monitor vireo populations (Rothstein and Cook 2000). Drainages with complex land ownership have successfully coordinated conservation efforts, however, as demonstrated at the Santa Ana River within southern California's largest coastal watershed, where a partnership among multiple agencies, organizations, and private citizens (e.g. Santa Ana River Watershed Alliance) effectively coordinates funding, implementation, and monitoring of management to benefit vireos and their habitats; since the group's inception in 1995, vireo numbers have climbed steadily. The Santa Ana River Watershed Alliance provides an encouraging model of what shared commitment and cooperation can bring to endangered species management, and exemplifies the iterative adaptive management processes involving planning, implementation, monitoring, evaluation, and refinement of management approaches needed to lead us closer to our goal of recovery.

Acknowledgments

It is a pleasure to acknowledge and thank the many dedicated field assistants who monitored vireos and sampled vegetation over the years, including P. M. Ashfield, P. P. Beck, J. Bennett, E. M. Berryman, M. M. Caruana, D. M. Evans, J. F. Falcone, S. C. Howard, H. L. Howitt, D. A. Kisner, V. J. Marquez, J. M. Newman, R. Y. Owens, D. L. Parker-Chapman, B. L. Peterson, J. K. Rombouts, J. W. Rourke, G. M. Shultz, E. A. Sgariglia, B. L. Sharp, M. O. Spiegelberg, J. L. Turnbull, M. J. Wellik, and J. M. Wells. Comments by C.J. Ralph and three anonymous reviewers improved the manuscript. Funds supporting this research have been provided by the California Department of Transportation, District 11; Marine Corps Base Camp Pendleton; and U.S. Army Corps of Engineers, Los Angeles District.

Fighting Fire with Fire: Bird Responses to Ponderosa Pine Treatments

Steve Zack

Abstract

Ponderosa pine (*Pinus ponderosa*) forests have been dramatically altered by a century of fire suppression, logging, and overgrazing. Many bird species associated with these forests have declined. We have little information on how bird communities interact with natural high-frequency, low-intensity fire regimes in these forests, and have gained almost all of our natural history information during the time of fire suppression. We are beginning to understand how birds respond to experimental treatments intended to return the open-stand structure of eastside ponderosa pine forests. Birds that forage on bark are associated with more open forests with fire, while birds that forage on foliage are more tied to the dense ponderosa forests of today caused by fire suppression. Returning fire to forests may help re-establish key processes such as the interactions of woodpeckers, bark beetles, wood-boring beetles, and fungi that create snags and cavity-nesting birds.

Introduction

Ponderosa pine (*Pinus ponderosa*) forests on the east side of the Cascade and Sierra mountains arguably have changed in structure and function in ways more profound than any other forests in western North America (Brown et al. 2004). A century of management has focused on fire suppression in these forests that historically saw frequent, low-intensity fire. This management has had profound effects on the structure and composition of these forests, transforming them from open-park like forests to closed forests, dense with shrubs and small trees that are drier in the southwest, more humid in the interior west and northwest. Intensive logging, particularly of large trees, and intensive grazing by domestic cattle have also been forces of change. Fire suppression increased encroachment by true firs (*Abies* spp.) and Douglas-firs (*Pseudotsuga menziesii*). This transformation of forest structure and composition has left them at risk of catastrophic fire. Today, with an ongoing drought fueled in part by climate change, these forests are the setting for many large-scale, stand-replacing fires (Westerling et al. 2006).

Birds in ponderosa pine forests have been affected by these changes in habitat. White-headed Woodpeckers (*Picoides albolarvatus*), Olive-sided Flycatchers (*Contopus cooperi*), and White-breasted Nuthatches (*Sitta carolinensis*) are among the birds associated with these forests that are considered to be in decline (Raphael et al. 1998, Saab and Powell 2005, Robertson and Hutto 2007). In general, it seems clear that fire-prone western forests are represented best by "bark-gleaning" birds (birds that forage on the bark, like woodpeckers, nuthatches and creepers), while fire-suppressed forests are typified by foliage-gleaning birds (e.g. warblers, tanagers, and vireos) (Saab and Powell 2005). It is important to point out that since fire suppression in this forest type has been the norm for the past century, our knowledge of the ecology of birds and other wildlife in ponderosa pine forests with intact fire histories is very limited. Virtually all studies of wildlife come from forests that have been altered by fire suppression. Thus, we have a very poor sense of bird communities in ponderosa pine with frequent fire, and the forest processes that result from fire and an open forest structure (Noss et al. 2006).

Confronting the extreme fire hazard of today's ponderosa pine forests is important to nearby communities and to the vitality of the forests themselves (Agee and Skinner 2005). The belated recognition that our "Smoky the Bear" culture of putting out every fire has paradoxically increased fire hazard in ponderosa forests, and has made clear the need to manage these forests in ways that may reduce such hazard. Understanding the ecological and societal consequences of doing so is among the most pressing issues in forest management today.

Project Introduction

In 1995, I joined an ad-hoc inter-disciplinary team of U.S. Forest Service scientists from the Pacific Southwest (California) research stations (Oliver and Powers 1998). This group had developed a series of experimental forest treatments availed by Blacks Mountain Experimental Forest (BMEF) in the Lassen National Forest, a ponderosa pine and white fir forest largely that did not experience the wide-scale logging of most all other forests, yet like all others was nonetheless subject to fire suppression.

BMEF is a rare forest with many large, living ponderosa pines, and abundant large snags (Zack et al. 2002; Fig. 1).

Forest Service scientists devised a contrasting study design at BMEF: experimentally thinning forests to 1) leave both complex horizontal and vertical forest structure (similar to what was presumed to be typical of historical forests) with large trees present, and 2) forest thinning for even-age management and with large trees removed (typical of many logged, managed forests today). Both treatments have replicates with prescribed fire, and treatments with no fire implemented. This study then provided an opportunity to examine the response of the bird community to an experimentally thinned ponderosa pine forest with large trees present, and to contrast treatments with and without prescribed fire.

In 1996 this same group took advantage of an opportunity to experimentally evaluate different means of accelerating late-successional forest structure in ponderosa pine/ white fir forests and reduce heavy white fir encroachment in the east side of the Klamath National Forest near Mt. Shasta (Ritchie and Harcksen 1999). This site is the Goosenest Adaptive Management Area (GAMA), which falls within the Northwest Forest Plan (Fig. 1). The result is a replicated design with and without prescribed fire. Controls (no treatments and continued fire suppression) provided the setting to evaluate the differences resulting from treatments.

Treatments at BMEF began in 1996 and at GAMA in 1997. Both provided a rare and important opportunity to experimentally evaluate wildlife response to the return of fire and the opened forest structure in ponderosa pine forests (George and Zack 2001), in part because the treatment units were large, 40 ha or larger.

Management Goals

The management goals of these two projects are: to explore ecological, economic, and potential societal consequences of different silvicultural treatments undertaken to return forest structure and function as it was presumed to be prior to fire suppression. The experimental nature of these efforts to restore forest structure to historical condition affords a clear opportunity to contrast the treatments with and without prescribed fire. The treatments were not directed at specific wildlife species in particular,

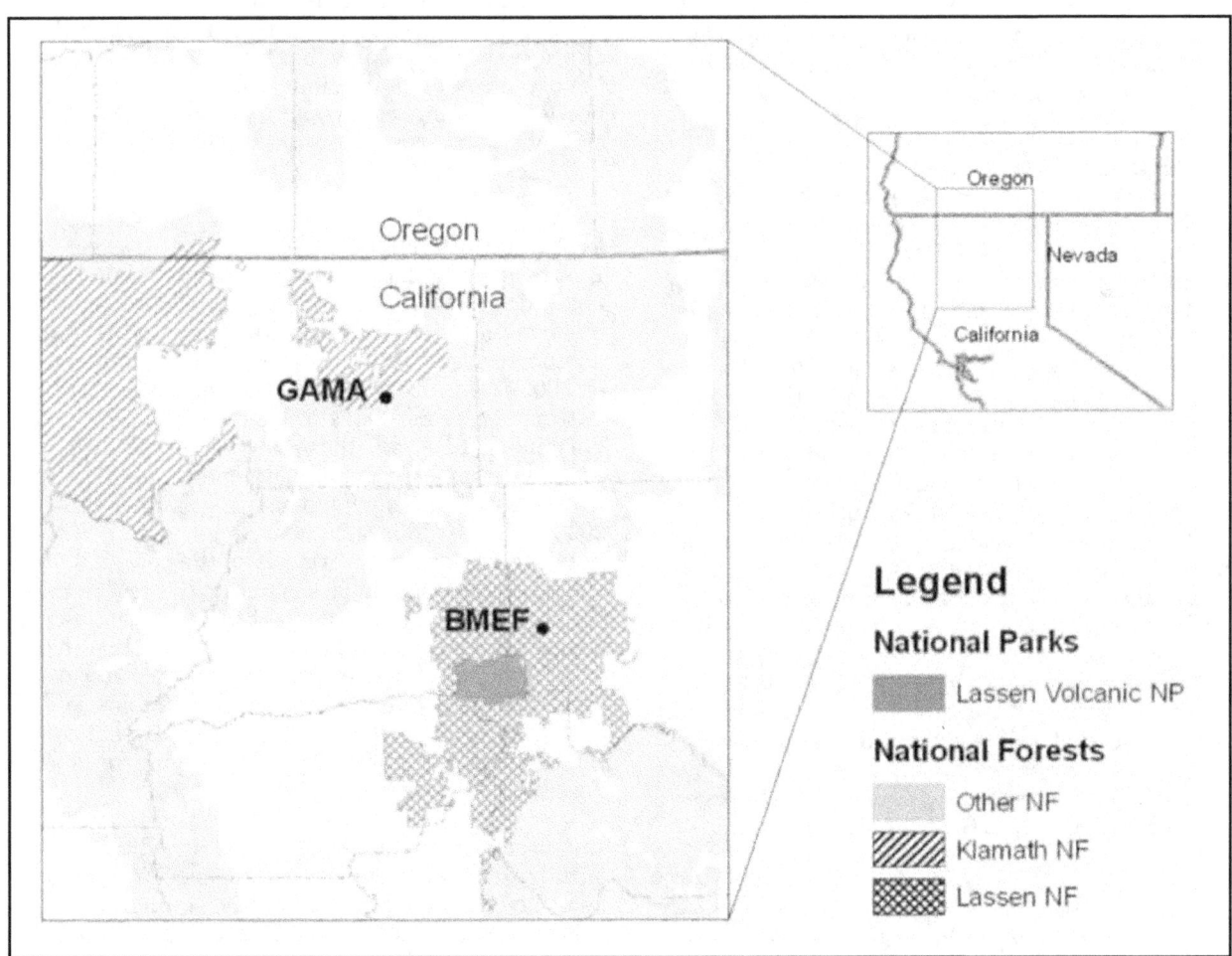

Figure 1. Location of the Goosenest Adaptive Management Area (GAMA) and Blacks Mountain Experimental Forest (BMEF).

but rather to explore experimental efforts that reconstruct historic forest structure and function, and so wildlife response is primarily viewed in that context (Zack et al. 1999).

Monitoring Regime
We deployed standardized point counts across all experimental units (and controls) prior to and after treatments. Point counts have generally been conducted every other year post-treatment at both sites. We have also extensively searched for and monitored nests. At GAMA we spot-mapped key species in an effort to contrast treatment effects.

Several side projects, primarily conducted by Humboldt State University grad students, have investigated detailed responses of individual bird species to the treatments. We also compared snag densities, sizes, and use by nesting birds at BMEF and GAMA prior to treatments (Zack et al. 2002). In addition, we have completed an extensive effort at GAMA of capture-recapture of small mammals (Converse et al. 2006; S.Z. and T.L. George, pers. comm.). The complex interactions of woodpeckers, bark beetles and wood borers, snags, and fungi that decay snags, and how those interactions may lead to potential cavity excavation were closely investigated (Farris et al. 2002, Farris et al. 2004, Farris and Zack 2005). These efforts were conducted at BMEF and in separate experimental treatments in the Ochoco National Forest of Oregon.

Responses to Management
In general, we are seeing differences by broad feeding guilds at both sites (George et al. 2005, George and Zack 2008). "Bark-gleaners," those birds that gain most of their prey by feeding on, or probing into the bark of conifers, seem associated with more open, large-tree forests. Bark gleaners include Black-Backed Woodpeckers (*Picoides arcticus*), White-breasted and Pygmy (*Sitta pygmaea*) nuthatches, Black-capped (*Poecile atracapilla*) and Mountain (*Poecile gambelli*) chickadees, and Brown Creepers (*Certhia americana*). White-headed Woodpeckers and White-breasted Nuthatches are both more common at BMEF; presumably because of the large trees and snags there (Zack et al. 2002, George et al. 2005). "Foliage-gleaners", those species that gain their food from needles of conifers, tend to be more common in the denser forest settings typical of GAMA. For example, Western Tanagers (*Piranga ludoviciana*) have responded negatively to the treatments at BMEF, and are more common in the "control" plots at GAMA in comparison to treated plots (George et al. 2005; S.Z. and T. L. George, pers. comm.).

There are many species-specific, and often site-specific responses, apart from the general pattern above. For example, White-headed Woodpeckers and White-breasted Nuthatches, appeared on burn treatments at GAMA where none were detected at that site before; Olive-sided Flycatchers, a species which sallies out to forage on aerial insects from high perches, are only observed on burned units at GAMA (reflecting the need to sort out other ecological features other than fire to explain their response); and American Robins (*Turdus migratorius*), a ground-foraging species, showed strong response at BMEF to both forest thinning and fire (George and Zack 2008). Dark-eyed Juncos (*Junco hyemalis*) reacted to prescribed fires at GAMA by nesting in trees with ground cover burned, reflecting a novel nesting response (Sperry et al. 2008).

An interesting interdependence between woodpeckers, bark beetles, and wood decaying fungi has emerged from this research (Farris et al. 2002, Farris et al. 2004). In ponderosa pine, cavities are excavated in the enlarged sapwood, unlike most other conifers where it is the heartwood that contains excavated cavities. Woodpeckers foraging on bark beetles and wood boring beetles that infest recently killed trees (snags), have wood-decaying fungi on their beaks (Farris et al. 2004). Thus, woodpeckers could facilitate the spread of fungi that decay sapwood, increasing the likelihood that snags they forage on decay rapidly and permit cavity excavation. Further, as bark beetles are drawn to fire-killed trees, that, in turn, quickly attract woodpeckers, it seems likely that the reintroduction of fire to ponderosa pine forests reinstalls an important set of interactions between woodpeckers, beetles, and fungi that result in snags with cavities, a crucial resource for many species of wildlife (Farris and Zack 2005).

Implementation of Results
In the fall of 2002, the Cone Fire surrounding the environs of BMEF made clear the main benefit of undertaking silvicultural treatments with thinning and prescribed fire in ponderosa pine (Skinner et al. 2005). This fire, after burning the surrounding untreated forests, died at the edge of the thin-burn plots at BMEF (those that had prescribed fires) or became a low-intensity understory fire (on plots with thinning and no fire) (Skinner et al. 2005). Many wildfires in the west have brought the public to recognize the urgency of the potential for catastrophic fires that risk communities and forests; the Cone Fire's interaction with BMEF treatments suggested a solution (Skinner et al. 2005), and that is to "fight fire with fire", and return the historic structure back to these forests. The combination of thinning and prescribed fire helps jump-start the re-creation of the way ponderosa pine forests "worked" a century ago.

It is premature to suggest that the benefits of such treatments to (some) wildlife species will be a driver in implementing such treatments. Clearly, woodpeckers, particularly Black-backed Woodpeckers and Hairy Woodpeckers (*Picoides villosus*), respond quickly to fire, or more precisely, to the wood-boring and bark beetles attracted by the fire.

Managing these ponderosa pine forests in ways that return the historical structure and processes to them is essential in maintaining them as forests dominated by ponderosa pine forest. By examining the contrasting forests (e.g. open ponderosa pine and encroached mixed-conifer) experimentally, we have been participating in a process that informs forest managers how best, and with what ecological consequences, to manage ponderosa pine. For Partners in Flight concerns, many western coniferous birds, particularly species like White-headed Woodpeckers and White-breasted Nuthatches, would benefit from widespread application of thinning and prescribed fire in ponderosa pine, assuming that large-trees are spared the thinning.

Conclusion

Confronting the risk of catastrophic fire in ponderosa pine forests is a monumental challenge, particularly when one considers the immense spatial scale of the problem. It is a problem which results from over a century of forest mismanagement. Implementing aggressive thinning and fire management now, however, is complex even across small landscape scales. Managing the ponderosa pine forests of today requires close attention to the forest structure details that require manipulation to reduce fire hazard (Agee and Skinner 2005), a strong sense of the regional context for forest structure in relation to adjacent forests and their fire susceptibilities (Brown et al. 2004), and a strong commitment by land managers to employ natural processes such as fire as a management tool and to understand wildlife benefits of doing so (Noss et al. 2006).

In collaboration with our U.S. Forest Service partners, we have begun to put a wildlife perspective on forest management. As our team brings forth different perspectives from the different disciplines they represent, we hope to continue to act as information brokers on this crucial issue in western forests.

Acknowlegments

Kerry Farris, T. Luke George, and William F. Laudenslayer have helped me understand wildlife issues in western forests through collaboration and friendship. Carl Skinner and Scott Stephens have shaped my thinking about fire in forests. The U.S. Forest Service partners include William F. Laudenslayer, Jr., Carl Skinner, Phil Weatherspoon, Pat Shea, William Oliver, and Martin Ritchie. Kerry Farris, and T. Luke George have been my major wildlife collaborator. Several graduate students from HSU, as well as dozens of field assistants, have all contributed to this diverse effort and brought their energy and enthusiasm to these studies. Support came from the U S. Forest Service, the Joint Fire Science Program, the Disney Foundation, and the Wildlife Conservation Society.

Literature Cited

Ackers, S., M. Brock, D.K. Fuhrmann, J. Gibson, T. Hofstra, L. Johnson, J. Roth, D. Sarr, and E. Starkey. 2002. A study plan to inventory vascular plants and vertebrates: Klamath Network. Department of the Interior, National Park Service, and Klamath Network, Ashland, Oregon. <http://science.nature.nps.gov/im/units/klmn/Inventories/Documents/Klamath_Network_Inventory_Study_Plan01.31.02.pdf> (29 April 2010).

Agee, J.K., and C.N. Skinner. 2005. Basic principles of fuel reduction treatments. Forest Ecology and Management 211:83-96.

Airola, D., and R. Barret. 1985. Foraging and habitat relationships of insect-gleaning birds in a Sierra Nevada mixed conifer forest. Condor 87:205-216.

Alaback, P.B., and F.R. Herman. 1988. Long-term response of understory vegetation to stand density in *Picea-Tsuga* forests. Canadian Journal of Forest Research 18:1522–1530.

Alexander, J.D. 1999. Bird-habitat relationships in the Klamath/Siskiyou mountains. M.S. thesis, Southern Oregon University, Ashland.

Alexander, J.D., C.J. Ralph, K. Hollinger, and B. Hogoboom. 2004. Using a wide-scale landbird monitoring network to determine landbird distribution and productivity in the Klamath Bioregion. Pages 33-41 *in* K.L. Mergenthaler, J.E. Williams, and E.S. Jules, editors. Proceedings of the second conference on Klamath-Siskiyou ecology. Siskiyou Field Institute, Cave Junction, Oregon.

Alexander, J.D., N.E. Seavy, and P.E. Hosten. 2007. Using conservation plans and bird monitoring to evaluate ecological effects of management: an example with fuels reduction activities in southwest Oregon. Forest Ecology and Management 238:375-383.

Altman, B. 1999. Conservation strategy for landbirds in coniferous forests of western Oregon and Washington. Oregon-Washington Partners in Flight and American Bird Conservancy, Corvallis, Oregon. <http://www.orwapif.org/pdf/western_forest.pdf> (13 July 2009).

Altman, B. 2000a. Conservation strategy for landbirds in lowlands and valleys of western Oregon and Washington. Oregon-Washington Partners in Flight and American Bird Conservancy, Boring, Oregon. <http://www.orwapif.org/pdf/western_lowlands.pdf> (12 November 2006).

Altman, B. 2000b. Conservation strategy for landbirds in the Northern Rocky Mountains of eastern Oregon and Washington. Oregon-Washington Partners in Flight and American Bird Conservancy, Corvallis, Oregon. <http://www.orwapif.org/pdf/northern_rockies.pdf> (13 July 2009).

Altman, B. 2000c. Conservation strategy for landbirds of the eastern slope of the Cascade mountains in Oregon and Washington. Oregon-Washington Partners in Flight and American Bird Conservancy, Corvallis, Oregon. <http://www.orwapif.org/pdf/east_slope.pdf> (13 July 2009).

Altman, B., and J. C. Hagar. 2006. Rainforest birds: a land manager's guide to breeding bird habitat in young conifer forests in the Pacific Northwest. U.S. Department of Interior, Geological Survey, Scientific Investigations Report 2006-5304, Reston, Virginia.

Anthony, R.G., E.D. Forsman, A.B. Franklin, D.R. Anderson, K.P. Burnham, G.C. White, C.J. Schwarz, J.D. Nichols, J.E. Hines, G.S. Olson, and others. 2006. Status and trends in demography of Northern Spotted Owls, 1985-2003. Wildlife Monographs 163:1-48.

Artman, V.L. 1990. Breeding bird populations and vegetation characteristics in commercially thinned and unthinned western hemlock forests of Washington. M.S. thesis, University of Washington, Seattle.

Bailey, J.D., C. Mayrsohn, P.S. Doescher, E. St. Pierre, and J.C. Tappeiner. 1998. Understory vegetation in old and young Douglas-fir forests of western Oregon. Forest Ecology and Management 112:289–302.

Baird, K. 1989. High quality restoration of riparian ecosystems. Restoration and Management Notes 7:60-64.

Baird, K.L., and J.P. Rieger. 1989. A restoration design for least Bell's vireo habitat in San Diego County. Pages 462-467 *in* D.L. Abell, technical coordinator. Proceedings of the California Riparian Systems Conference: protection, management, and restoration for the 1990's; September 22-24, 1988. U.S. Department of Agriculture, Forest Service, General Technical Report PSW-110, Davis, California.

Ballard, G., G.R. Guepel, N. Nur, and T. Gardali. 2003. Long-term declines and decadal patterns in population trends of songbirds in western North America, 1979–1999. Condor 105:737-755.

Bartos, D.L. 2001. Landscape dynamics of aspen and conifer forest. Pages 5-14 *in* W.D. Shepperd, D. Binkley, D.L. Bartos, T.J. Stohlgren, and L.G. Eskew, compilers. Sustaining aspen in Western landscapes: symposium proceedings. U.S. Department of Agriculture, Forest Service, Rocky Mountain Research Station, General Technical Report RMRS-P-18, Grand Junction, Colorado.

Beedy, E. 1981. Bird communities and forest structure in the Sierra Nevada of California. Condor 83:97-105.

Bonney, R., D.N. Pashley, R.J. Cooper, and L. Niles, editors. 1999. Strategies for bird conservation: the Partners in Flight planning process. Cornell Lab of Ornithology, Ithaca, New York. <http://birds.cornell.edu/pifcapemay> (17 November 2006).

Bosch, O.J.H., A.H. Ross, and R.J.S. Beeton. 2003. Integrating science and management through collaborative learning and better information management. Systems Research and Behavioral Science 20:107-118.

Brand, L.A., and T.L. George. 2001. Response of passerine birds to forest edge in Coast Redwood forest fragments. Auk 118:678-686.

Brower, J.E., J.H. Zar, and C.N. von Ende. 1990. Field and laboratory methods for general ecology. 3rd ed. Wm. C. Brown Publishers, Dubuque, Iowa.

Brown, E.R., technical editor. 1985. Management of wildlife and fish habitats in forests of western Oregon and Washington. U.S. Department of Agriculture, Forest Service, Pacific Northwest Region, Publication No. R6-F&WL-192-1985, Portland, Oregon.

Brown, R.T., J.K. Agee, and J.F. Franklin. 2004. Forest restoration and fire: principles in the context of place. Conservation Biology 18:903-912.

Brown, S., C. Hickey, B. Harrington, and R. Gill. 2001. United States shorebird conservation plan, 2nd edition. Manomet Center for Conservation Sciences, Manomet, Massachusetts.

Brush, T., and E.W. Stiles. 1986. Using food abundance to predict habitat use by birds. Pages 57–63 *in* J. Verner, M.L. Morrison, and C.J. Ralph, editors. Wildlife 2000: modeling habitat relationships of terrestrial vertebrates. University of Wisconsin Press, Madison, Wisconsin.

Buckland, S.T., D.R. Anderson, K.P. Burnham, and J.L. Laake. 1993. Distance sampling: estimating abundance of biological populations. Chapman and Hall, London, United Kingdom.

Burnett, R.D., and D.L. Humple. 2003. Songbird monitoring in the Lassen National Forest: results from the 2002 Field Season with summaries of 6 years of data (1997-2002). Unpublished report. U.S. Department of Agriculture, U.S. Forest Service, Lassen National Forest, California.

Burnett, R.D., T. Gardali, and G.R. Geupel. 2005. Using songbird monitoring to help guide and evaluate salmonid focused stream rehabilitations projects. Pages 533-536 *in* C.J. Ralph and T.D. Rich, editors. Bird conservation implementation and integration in the Americas: proceedings of the Third International Partners in Flight Conference, 2002 March 20-24; Asilomar, California. U.S. Department of Agriculture, Forest Service, Pacific Southwest Research Station, General Technical Report PSW-GTR-191, Albany, California.

California Partners in Flight [CalPIF]. 2002a. The oak woodland bird conservation plan: a strategy for protecting and managing oak woodland habitats and associated birds in California, v. 2.0. Point Reyes Bird Observatory, Stinson Beach, California. <http://www.prbo.org/calpif/plans.html> (16 July 2009).

California Partners in Flight [CalPIF]. 2002b. Draft coniferous forest bird conservation plan: a strategy for protecting and managing coniferous forest habitats and associated birds in California, v. 1.0. Point Reyes Bird Observatory, Stinson Beach, California. <http://www.prbo.org/calpif/pdfs/conifer.v-1.pdf> (12 November 2006).

Carey, A.B., D.R. Thysell, and A.W. Brodie. 1999. The forest ecosystem study: background, rationale, implementation, baseline conditions, and silvicultural assessment. U.S. Department of Agriculture, Forest Service, Pacific Northwest Research Station, General Technical Report PNW-GTR-457, Portland, Oregon

Chambers, C.L. 1996. Response of terrestrial vertebrates to three silvicultural treatments in the central Oregon Coast Range. Ph.D. dissertation, Oregon State University, Corvallis.

Chang, C. 1996. Ecosystem responses to fire and variations in fire regimes. Pages 1071-1099 *in* Sierra Nevada Ecosystem Project, Final report to Congress, Vol. II, assessments and scientific basis for management options. Centers for Water and Wildland Resources, University of California, Davis, California.

Chase, M.K., and G.R. Geupel. 2005. The use of avian focal species for conservation planning in California. Pages 130-142 *in* C.J. Ralph and T.D. Rich, editors. Bird conservation implementation and integration in the Americas: proceedings of the Third International Partners in Flight Conference, 2002 March 20-24; Asilomar, California. U.S. Department of Agriculture, Forest Service, Pacific Southwest Research Station, General Technical Report PSW-GTR-191, Albany, California.

Converse, S.J., G.C. White, K.L. Farris, and S. Zack. 2006. Small mammal responses to forest fuel reduction: national-scale responses to fire and fire surrogates. Ecological Applications 16:1717-1729.

Covington, W.W., and M.M. Moore. 1994. Post-settlement changes in natural fire regimes and forest structure: ecological restoration of old growth ponderosa pine forests. Pages 153-181 *in* R.N. Sampson and D.L. Adams, editors. Assessing forest ecosystem health in the inland west. The Haworth Press, Binghamton, New York.

Crane M.F. 1990. *Pteridium aquilinum*. *In* Fire Effects Information System [Online]. U.S. Department of Agriculture, Forest Service, Rocky Mountain Research Station, Fire Sciences Laboratory, General Technical Report RMRS-GTR-42, Fort Collins, Colorado. <http://www.fs.fed.us/database/feis/> (23 June 2009).

Crawford, H.S., and D.T. Jennings. 1989. Predation by birds on spruce budworm *Choristoneura fumifernana:* functional, numerical, and total responses. Ecology 70:152-163.

Curtis, R.O., D.S. DeBell, C.A. Harrington, D.P. Lavender, J.B. St. Clair, J.C. Tappeiner II, and J.D. Walstad. 1998. Silviculture for multiple objectives in the Douglas-fir region. U.S. Department of Agriculture, Forest Service, Pacific Northwest Research Station, General Technical Report PNW-GTR-435, Portland, Oregon.

DellaSala, D.A., S.T. Reid, T.J. Frest, J.R. Strittholt, and D.M. Olson. 1999. A global perspective on the biodiversity of the Klamath-Siskiyou ecoregion. Natural Areas Journal 19:300-319.

DeSante, D.F., K.M. Burton, J.F. Saracco, and B.L. Walker. 1995. Productivity indices and survival rate estimates from MAPS, a continent-wide program of constant-effort mist netting in North America. Journal Applied Statistics 22:935-947.

DeSante, D.F., K.M. Burton, P. Velez, D. Froehlich, and D.R. Kaschube. 2010. MAPS manual: 2010 protocol. Unpublished report. Contribution No. 127 of The Institute for Bird Populations, Point Reyes Station, California.

DeSante, D.F., and M.P. Nott. 2001. An overview of the North American Monitoring Avian Productivity and Survivorship (MAPS) program. EURING Newsletter 3. Istituto Nazionale per la Fauna Selvetica "Alessandro Ghigi". <http://www.euring.org/about_euring/newsletter3/index.html> (June 4, 2010).

DeSante, D.F., J.F. Saracco, P. Pyle, D.R. Kaschube, and M.K. Chambers. 2008. Integrating the MAPS program into Coordinated Bird Monitoring in the Northeast (U.S. Fish and Wildlife Service Region 5). Unpublished report. The Institute for Bird Populations, Point Reyes Station, California.

Dillingham, C. 2003. Orange-crowned warbler *Vermivora celata*. Pages 503–505 *in* Marshall, D.B., M.G. Hunter, and A. Contreras, editors. Birds of Oregon: a general reference. Oregon State University Press, Corvallis, Oregon.

Doolittle, A.M. 2000. Arthropod communities on understory plants in thinned and unthinned Douglas-fir forests in the Oregon Coast Range. M.S. thesis, Oregon State University, Corvallis.

Dowlan, S.G. 2003. MacGillivray's warbler *Oporornis tomiei*. Pages 522–524 *in* D.B. Marshall, M.G. Hunter, and A. Contreras, editors. Birds of Oregon: a general reference. Oregon State University Press, Corvallis, Oregon.

Dunn, E.H., and C.J. Ralph. 2004. Use of mist nets as a tool for bird population monitoring. Studies in Avian Biology 29:1-6.

Earnst, S.L., J. Ballard, and D.L. Dobkin. 2005. Riparian songbird abundance a decade after cattle removal on Hart Mountain and Sheldon National Wildlife Refuges. Pages 550-558 *in* C.J. Ralph and T.D. Rich, editors. Bird conservation implementation and integration in the Americas: proceedings of the Third International Partners in Flight Conference, 2002 March 20-24; Asilomar, CA. U.S. Department of Agriculture, Forest Service, Pacific Southwest Research Station, General Technical Report PSW-GTR-191, Albany, California.

Endangered Species Act. 1973. Public Law No. 03-205., 87 U.S. Statutes at Large 884 (December 23, 1973) (Codified and amended at 16 U.S.C. secs. 1531-1543).

Falxa, G.A., J. Baldwin, D. Lynch, S.K. Nelson, S.L. Miller, S.F. Pearson, M.G. Raphael, C. Strong, T. Bloxton, B. Galleher, and others. 2009. Marbled Murrelet effectiveness monitoring, Northwest Forest Plan: 2008 summary report. Unpublished report. The Interagency Regional Monitoring Program. Arcata, California. <http://www.reo.gov/monitoring/reports/murrelet/MAMU_2008_EM_summary_report.pdf> (June 10, 2010).

Farris, K.L, E.O. Garton, P.J. Heglund, S. Zack, and P.J. Shea. 2002. Woodpecker foraging and the successional decay of ponderosa pine. Pages 237-246 in W.F. Laudenslayer, Jr., P.J. Shea, B.E. Valentine, P.C. Weatherspoon and T.E. Lisle, technical coordinators. Proceedings of the symposium on the ecology and management of dead wood in western forests. U.S. Department of Agriculture, Forest Service, Pacific Southwest Research Station, General Technical Report PSW-GTR-181, Albany, California.

Farris, K.L., M.J. Huss, and S. Zack. 2004. The role of foraging woodpeckers in decomposition of ponderosa pine snags. Condor 106:50-59.

Farris, K.L., and S. Zack. 2005. Woodpecker-snag interactions: an overview of current knowledge in ponderosa pine systems. Pages 183-196 in M. Ritchie, D.A. Maguire, and A. Youngblood, editors. Proceedings of the symposium on ponderosa pine: issues, trends, and management. U.S. Department of Agriculture, Forest Service, Pacific Southwest Research Station, General Technical Report PSW-GTR-198, Albany, California.

Finch, D., and P. Stangel, editors. 1993. Status and management of neotropical migrant birds: proceedings of the Estes Park Partners in Flight conference. U.S. Department of Agriculture, Forest Service, General Technical Report GTR-RM-229, Fort Collins, Colorado.

Flack, J.A.D. 1976. Bird populations of aspen forest in western North America. Ornithological Monographs 19:1-97.

Fleischner, T.L. 1994. Ecological costs of livestock grazing in western North America. Conservation Biology 8:629-644.

Forest Ecosystem Management Assessment Team. 1993. Forest ecosystem management: an ecological, economic, and social assessment. U.S. Department of Agriculture, Forest Service, U.S. Department of the Interior, Fish and Wildlife Service, Bureau of Land Management, and National Park Service, U.S. Department of Commerce, National Oceanic and Atmospheric Administration and National Marine Fisheries Service, and Environmental Protection Agency. Portland, Oregon.

Franklin, J.F., and C.T. Dyrness. 1988. The natural vegetation of Oregon and Washington. Oregon State University Press, Corvallis, Oregon.

Franzreb, K.E. 1989. Ecology and conservation of the endangered Least Bell's Vireo. U.S. Department of Interior, Fish and Wildlife Service, Biological Report 89:17.

Frey, R.I., K.W. Larson, and J.D. Alexander. 2007. Report to the National Park Service Klamath Network on bird monitoring efforts by the Klamath Bird Observatory in the Oregon Caves National Monument 2002-2006. Unpublished report. Klamath Bird Observatory, Ashland, Oregon. <http://science.nature.nps.gov/im/units/klmn/Inventories/Birds/KBO_Birds.cfm> (23 July 2009).

Gardali, T., A.L. Holmes, S.L. Small, N. Nur, G.R. Geupel, and G.H. Golet. 2006. Abundance patterns of landbirds in restored and remnant riparian forests on the Sacramento River, California, U.S.A. Restoration Ecology 14:391-403.

Garrett, K.L., M.G. Raphael, and R.D. Dixon. 1996. White-headed Woodpecker (Picoides albolarvatus). In A. Poole and F. Gill, editors. The birds of North America, No. 252. The Academy of Natural Sciences, Philadelphia, Pennsylvania; American Ornithologists' Union, Washington, D.C.

George, T.L. and L.A. Brand. 2002. The effects of habitat fragmentation on birds in coast redwood forests. Studies in Avian Biology 25:92-102.

George, T.L., and S. Zack. 2001. Spatial and temporal considerations in restoring habitat for wildlife. Restoration Ecology 9:272-279.

George, T.L., and S. Zack. 2008. Response of forest birds to manipulation of forest structure and prescribed fire at Black's Mountain Experimental Forest. Canadian Journal of Forestry Research 38:936-942.

George, T.L., S. Zack, and W.F. Laudenslayer Jr. 2005. A comparison of bird species composition and abundance between mid- and late-seral ponderosa pine forests. Pages 159-170 in M. Ritchie, D.A. Maguire, and A. Youngblood, editors. Proceedings of the symposium on ponderosa pine: issues, trends, and management. U.S. Department of Agriculture, Forest Service, Pacific Southwest Research Station, General Technical Report PSW-GTR-198, Albany, California.

Graber, J.W., and R.R. Graber. 1983. Feeding rates of warblers in spring. Condor 85:139–150.

Griffith, J.T., and J.C. Griffith. 2000. Cowbird control and the endangered Least Bell's Vireo: a management success story. Pages 342-356 *in* J.N.M. Smith, T.L. Cook, S.I. Rothstein, S.K. Robinson, and S.G. Sealy, editors. Ecology and management of cowbirds and their hosts. University of Texas Press, Austin, Texas.

Grinnell, J. and A. Miller. 1944. The distribution of the birds of California. Pacific Coast Avifauna 27. Contribution from the Museum of Vertebrate Zoology of the University of California. Cooper Ornithological Club, Berkeley, California.

Hagar, J.C. 2003a. Swainson's thrush *Catharus ustulatus*. Pages 481–483 *in* D.B. Marshall, M.G. Hunter, and A. Contreras, editors. Birds of Oregon: a general reference. Oregon State University Press, Corvallis, Oregon.

Hagar, J.C. 2003b. Wilson's warbler *Wilsonia pusilla*. Pages 526–528 *in* Marshall, D.B., M.G. Hunter, and A. Contreras, editors. Birds of Oregon: a general reference. Oregon State University Press, Corvallis, Oregon.

Hagar, J.C., K.M. Dugger, and E.E. Starkey. 2007. Arthropod prey of Wilson's Warblers in the understory of Douglas-fir forests. Wilson Journal of Ornithology 119:533-546.

Hagar, J.C., S. Howlin, and L.M. Ganio. 2004. Short-term response of songbirds to experimental thinning of young Douglas-fir forests in the Oregon Cascades. Forest Ecology and Management 199:333-347.

Hagar, J.C., W.C. McComb, and W.H. Emmingham. 1996. Bird communities in commercially thinned and unthinned Douglas-fir stands of western Oregon. Wildlife Society Bulletin 24:353-366.

Hammond, P.C., and J.C. Miller. 1998. Comparison of the biodiversity of Lepidoptera within three forested ecosystems. Annals of the Entomological Society of America 91:323–328.

Haney, A., and R.L. Power. 1996. Adaptive management for sound ecosystem management. Environmental Management 20:879-886.

Hansen, A.J., T.A. Spies, F.J. Swanson, and J.L. Ohmann. 1991. Conserving biodiversity in managed forests. BioScience 41:382-391.

Haveri, B.A., and A.B. Carey. 2000. Forest management strategy, spatial heterogeneity, and winter birds in Washington. Wildlife Society Bulletin 28:643-652.

Hayes, J.P., S.S. Chan, W.H. Emmingham, J.C. Tappeiner, II, L.D. Kellogg, and J.D. Bailey. 1997. Wildlife response to thinning young forests in the Pacific Northwest. Journal of Forestry 95:28-33.

Hayes J.P., J.M. Weikel, and M. Huso. 2003. Effects of commercial thinning on breeding birds in the northern Coast Range of Oregon. Ecological Applications 13:1222–1232.

Haynes, R.W., B.T. Bormann, D.C. Lee, and J.R. Martin, editors. 2006. Northwest Forest Plan—the first 10 years (1994-2003): synthesis of monitoring and research results. U.S. Department of Agriculture, Forest Service, Pacific Northwest Research Station, General Technical Report PNW-GTR-651, Portland, Oregon.

Hejl, S.J. 1994. Human induced changes in bird populations in coniferous forests in western North America during the past 100 years. Studies in Avian Biology 15:232-246.

Heltzel, J.M., and S.L. Earnst. 2006. Factors influencing nest success of songbirds in aspen and willow riparian areas in the Great Basin. Condor 108:842–855.

Holmes, R.T. 1990. Ecological and evolutionary impacts of bird predation on forest insects: an overview. Studies in Avian Biology 13:6–13.

Huff, M.H., M.G. Raphael, S.L. Miller, S.K. Nelson, and J. Baldwin, technical coordinators. 2006. Northwest Forest Plan—the first 10 years (1994-2003): status and trends of populations and nesting habitat for the Marbled Murrelet. U.S. Department of Agriculture, Forest Service, Pacific Northwest Research Station, General Technical Report PNW-GTR-650, Portland, Oregon.

Huffman D.W., J.C. Tappeiner II, and J.C. Zasada. 1994. Regeneration of salal (*Gaultheria shallon*) in the central Coast Range forests of Oregon. Canadian Journal of Botany 72:39-5.

Hutto, R.L. 1998. Using landbirds as an indicator species group. Page 75-92 *in* J.M. Marzluff and R. Sallabanks, editors. Avian conservation: research and management. Island Press, Covelo, California.

Jacobson, S.K., J.K. Morris, J.S. Sanders, E.N. Wiley, M. Brooks, R.E. Bennetts, H.F. Percival, and S. Marynowski. 2006. Understanding barriers to implementation of an adaptive land management program. Conservation Biology 20:1516-1527.

Jones, B.E., T.H. Rickman, A. Vasquez, Y. Sado, and K.W. Tate. 2005. Removal of invasive conifers to regenerate degraded aspen stands in the Sierra Nevada. Restoration Ecology 13:373-379.

Jones, J.R., and N.V. DeByle. 1985. Fire. Pages 78-81 *in* N.V. DeByle and R.P. Winokur, editors. Aspen: ecology and management in the western United States. U.S. Department of Agriculture, Forest Service, Rocky Mountain Forest and Range Experiment Station, General Technical Report RM-119, Fort Collins, Colorado.

Kay, C.E. 1997. Is aspen doomed? Journal of Forestry 95:4-11.

Keough, H.L., and D.J. Blahna. 2006. Achieving integrated, collaborative ecosystem management. Conservation Biology 20:1373-1382.

Klamath Bird Observatory and U.S. Bureau of Land Management. 2009. Riparian fuel treatments in intermittent and perennial stream riparian areas: effectiveness and ecological effects. Unpublished report. Klamath Bird Observatory, Rep. No. KBO-2009-0008. Ashland, Oregon.

Kreitinger, K., and J.K. Wood. 2005. Least Bell's Vireo nests in Stanislaus County: are they coming back? Central Valley Bird Club Bulletin 8:45-48.

Kus, B.E. 1998. Use of restored riparian habitat by the endangered Least Bell's Vireo (*Vireo bellii pusillus*). Restoration Ecology 6:75-82.

Kus, B.E., and M.J. Whitfield. 2005. Parasitism, productivity, and population growth: response of Least Bell's Vireos (*Vireo bellii pusillus*) and Southwestern Willow Flycatchers (*Empidonax traillii extimus*) to cowbird (*Molothrus* spp.) control. Ornithological Monographs 57:16-27.

Kushlan, J.A., M.J. Steinkamp, K.C. Parsons, J. Capp, M.A. Cruz, M. Coulter, I. Davidson, L. Dickson, N. Edelson, R. Elliot, and others. 2002. Waterbird conservation for the Americas: the North American Waterbird Conservation Plan, v.1. Waterbird Conservation for the Americas, Washington, D.C. <http://www.fs.fed.us/database/feis/> (19 April 2010).

Lambeck, R.J. 1997. Focal species: a multi-species umbrella for nature conservation. Conservation Biology 11:849-856.

Laymon, S.A. 1987. Brown-headed Cowbirds in California: historical perspectives and management opportunities in riparian habitats. Western Birds 18:63-70.

Leu, M. 2000. Breeding territory settlement patterns and mate choice in a monochromatic Tyrannid flycatcher. Ph.D. dissertation, University of Washington, Seattle.

Lint, J.B., technical coordinator. 2005. Northwest Forest Plan—The first 10 Years (1994-2003): status and trends of Northern Spotted Owl populations and habitat. U.S. Department of Agriculture, Forest Service, Pacific Northwest Research Station, General Technical Report PNW-GTR-648, Portland, Oregon.

Lint, J., B. Noon, R. Anthony, E. Forsman, M. Raphael, M. Collopy, and E. Starkey. 1999. Northern Spotted Owl effectiveness monitoring plan for the Northwest Forest Plan. U.S. Department of Agriculture, Forest Service, Pacific Northwest Research Station, General Technical Report PNW-GTR-440, Portland, Oregon.

Madsen, S., D. Evans, T. Hamer, P. Henson, S. Miller, S.K. Nelson, D. Roby, and M. Stapanian. 1999. Marbled Murrelet effectiveness monitoring plan for the Northwest Forest Plan. U.S. Department of Agriculture, Forest Service, Pacific Northwest Research Station, General Technical Report PNW-GTR-439, Portland, Oregon.

Manuwal, D.A. 1991. Spring bird communities in the southern Washington Cascade Range. Pages 145-160 *in* L.F. Ruggiero, K.B. Aubrey, A.B. Carey, and M.H. Huff, editors. Wildlife and vegetation of unmanaged Douglas-fir forests. U.S. Department of Agriculture Forest Service General Technical Report PNW-GTR-285, Portland, Oregon.

Marcot, B.G. 1984. Habitat relationships of birds in young-growth Douglas-fir in northwestern California. Ph.D. Dissertation, Oregon State University, Corvallis

Marshall, D., M. Hunter, and A. Contreras. 2003. The birds of Oregon: a general reference. Oregon State University Press, Corvallis, Oregon.

McComb, W.C., T.A. Spies, and W.H. Emmingham. 1993. Douglas-fir forests: managing for timber and mature-forest habitat. Journal of Forestry 91:31-42.

McConnell, T., E. Johnson, and B. Burns. 2000. A guide to conducting aerial sketchmap surveys. U.S. Department of Agriculture, Forest Service, Forest Health Technology Enterprise Team, FHTET 00-01, Fort Collins, Colorado.

McCullough, S. 2006. Inventory summary report: FY 2000-2004. Unpublished report. U.S. Department of the Interior, National Park Service, Klamath Network, Ashland, Oregon. <http://science.nature.nps.gov/im/units/klmn/Inventories/Documents/KLMN_Inventory_Summary_Report_Sarahfinal.pdf> (29 April 2010).

McGarigal, K., and B.J. Marks. 1995. FRAGSTATS: spatial pattern analysis program for quantifying landscape structure. U.S. Department of Agriculture Forest Service General Technical Report PNW-GTR-351, Portland, Oregon.

Miller, S.L., C.J. Ralph, M.G. Raphael, C. Strong, C.W. Thompson, J. Baldwin, M.H. Huff, and G.A. Falxa. 2006. At-sea monitoring of Marbled Murrelet population status and trend in the Northwest Plan area. Pages 31-60 *in* M.H Huff, M.G. Raphael, S.L. Miller, S.K. Nelson, and J. Baldwin, technical coordinators. Northwest Forest Plan—the first 10 years (1994-2003): status and trends of populations and nesting habitat for the Marbled Murrelet. U.S. Department of Agriculture, Forest Service, General Technical Report PNW-GTR-650, Portland, Oregon.

Mills, T.R., M.A. Rumble, and L.D. Flake. 2000. Habitat of birds in ponderosa pine and aspen/birch forests in the Black Hills. Journal of Field Ornithology 71:187-206.

Minnich, R.A., M.G. Barbour, J.H. Burk, and R.F. Fernau. 1995. Sixty years of change in California coniferous forests of the San Bernardino mountains. Conservation Biology 9:902-914.

Mitchell, M.S., S.H. Rutzmoser, T.B. Wigley, C. Loehle, J.A. Gerwin, P.D. Keyser, R.A. Lancia, R.W. Perry, C.L. Reynolds, R.E. Thill, and others. 2006. Relationships between avian richness and landscape structure at multiple scales using multiple landscapes. Forest Ecology and Management 221:155-169.

Moir, W.H., and W.M. Block. 2001. Adaptive management on public lands in the United States: commitment or rhetoric? Environmental Management 28:141-148.

Moller, A.P. 1991. Clutch size, nest predation, and distribution of avian unequal competitors in a patchy environment. Ecology 72:1336-1349.

Mueggler, W.F. 1985. Forage. Pages 129-134 *in* N.V. DeByle and R.P. Winokur, editors. Aspen: ecology and management in the Western United States. U.S. Department of Agriculture, Forest Service, Rocky Mountain Forest and Range Experiment Station, General Technical Report RM-119, Fort Collins, Colorado.

Muir, P.S., R.L. Mattingly, J.C. Tappeiner II, J.D. Bailey, W.E. Elliot, J.C. Hagar, J.C. Miller, E.B. Peterson, and E.E. Starkey. 2002. Managing for biodiversity in young Douglas-fir forests of western Oregon. U.S. Department of Interior, Geological Survey, Biological Resources Division, Biological Science Report USGS/BRD/BSR-2002-0006, Corvallis, Oregon.

National Park Service. 2006a. Chapter 4: natural resources in management policies. U.S. Department of Interior, National Park Service, Washington, D.C. <http://www.nps.gov/policy/mp2006.pdf> (29 April 2010).

National Park Service. 2006b. Prioritizing and selecting vital signs – what should be monitored? U.S. Department of Interior, National Park Service, Washington, D.C. <http://science.nature.nps.gov/im/monitor/VitalSigns.cfm> (29 April 2010).

National Park Service. 2008a. The inventory and monitoring program. U.S. Department of Interior, National Park Service, Washington, D.C. <http://science.nature.nps.gov/im/index.cfm> (29 April 2010).

National Park Service. 2008b. The Klamath Network inventory and monitoring program. U.S. Department of Interior, National Park Service, Washington, D.C. <http://science.nature.nps.gov/im/units/klmn/> (29 April 2010).

National Park Service. 2009. Certification of vascular and vertebrate species list for the NPS. U.S. Department of Interior, National Park Service, National Park Service Organic Act. 16 U.S.C 1-4 et seq. 1988. 25 August 1916. 39 Stat. 535, Washington, D.C. <http://science.nature.nps.gov/im/inventory/spplists/index.cfm> (29 April 2010).

National Land Cover Dataset. 1992. USGS, EROS Data Center. U.S. Department of Interior, Geological Survey, Washington, D.C. <http://edc.usgs.gov/products/landcover/nlcd.html> (22 July 2009)

Noon, B.R. and J.A. Blakesley. 2006. Conservation of the Northern Spotted Owl under the Northwest Forest Plan. Conservation Biology 20:288-296.

North American Waterfowl Management Plan Committee. 2004. North American Waterfowl Management Plan 2004. Implementation framework: strengthening the biological foundation. Canadian Wildlife Service, U.S. Department of Interior, Fish and Wildlife Service, and Secretaria de Medio Ambiente y Recursos Naturales, Washington, D.C. <http://www.fws.gov/birdhabitat/nawmp/files/ImplementationFramework.pdf> (9 June 2010).

Noss, R.F., P. Beier, W.W. Covington, R.E. Grumbine, D.B. Lindenmayer, J.W. Prather, F. Schmiegelow, T.D. Sisk, and D.J. Vosick. 2006. Recommendations for integrating restoration ecology and conservation biology in ponderosa pine of the southwestern United States. Restoration Ecology 14:4-10.

Nott, M.P. and M. Chambers. 2008. Monitoring, modeling, and managing landbird populations on Department of Defense lands. Unpublished report. Legacy Resources Management Office, Washington D.C. <http://www.birdpop.org/dod/dod_ibp.htm> (24 July 2009).

Nott, M.P. and D.F. DeSante. 2002a. Demographic monitoring and the identification of transients in mark-recapture models. Pages 727-736 *in* Scott, J.M., P.J. Heglund, M. Morrison, M. Raphael, J. Haufler, and B. Wall, editors. Predicting species occurrences: issues of scale and accuracy. Island Press, Covello, California.

Nott, M.P., and D.F. DeSante. 2002b. A proposed methodology for adjusting productivity indices given missing effort in constant-effort mist-netting data. Unpublished report. U.S. Department of Defense, Legacy Resources Management Office. Contribution No.163 of The Institute for Bird Populations, Point Reyes Station, California.

Nott, M.P., D.F. DeSante, P. Pyle, and N. Michel. 2005. Managing landbird populations in forests of the Pacific Northwest region. Unpublished report. U.S. Department of Agriculture, Forest Service, Pacific Northwest Region 6. Contribution No. 254 of The Institute for Bird Populations, Point Reyes Station, California. <http://www.birdpop.org/usfsr6/downloads/NWFFullReport.pdf> *(4 June 2010)*.

Nott, M.P., D.F. DeSante, R.B. Siegel, and P. Pyle. 2002. Influences of the El Niño/Southern Oscillation and the North Atlantic Oscillation on avian productivity in forests of the Pacific Northwest of North America. Global Ecology and Biogeography 11:333-342.

Nott, M.P., and D. Kaschube. 2007. Managing landbird populations in forests of the Pacific Northwest region. Web-based management decision-support tools for Pacific Northwest forest managers. Unpublished report. U.S. Department of Agriculture, Forest Service, Pacific Northwest Region 6. <http://www.birdpop.org/usfsr6/usfspnwr6.htm> (23 July 2009).

Nott, M.P., and N. Michel. 2005. Management strategies for reversing declines in landbirds of conservation concern on military installations: predictive modeling of landbird populations on military installations. Unpublished report. Legacy Resources Management Office. Washington D.C. Contribution No. 269, The Institute for Bird Populations, Point Reyes Station, California.

Nott, M.P. and T. Morris. 2007. Performance measure analysis: examples of comparing and contrasting installation-specific demographics with regional demographics and landscape characteristics. Unpublished report. Legacy Resources Management Office, Washington D.C. Contribution No. 324, The Institute for Bird Populations, Point Reyes Station, California.

Nyberg, B. 1999. Implementing adaptive management of British Columbia's forests: where have we gone wrong and right? Pages 25-28 *in* G.B. MacDonald, J. Fraser, and P. Gray, editors. Proceedings of the 1998 Provincial Science Forum. Adaptive management forum: linking management and science to achieve ecological sustainability, October 13-16, 1998. Science development and transfer series No. 001. Queen's Printer for Ontario, Ontario, Canada.

Oliver, W.W., and R.F. Powers. 1998. Blacks Mountain California: interdisciplinary field research in ponderosa pine. Journal of Forestry 96:4-9.

O'Neil, T.A., D.H. Johnson, C. Barrett, M. Trevithick, K.A. Bettinger, C. Kiilsgaard, M. Vander Heyden, E.L. Greda, D. Stinson, B.G. Marcot, and others. 2001. Matrixes for wildlife-habitat relationship in Oregon and Washington. CD in D.H. Johnson and T.A. O'Neil, managing directors. Wildlife-habitat relationships in Oregon and Washington. Northwest Habitat Institute., Oregon State University Press, Corvallis, Oregon.

Panjabi, A., C. Beardmore, P. Blancher, G. Butcher, M. Carter, D. Demarest, E. Dunn, C. Hunter, D. Pashley, K. Rosenberg, and others. 2001. The Partners in Flight handbook on species assessment and prioritization, v. 1.1. Rocky Mountain Bird Observatory, Brighton, Colorado. <http://www.rmbo.org/pubs/downloads/Handbook.pdf> (29 April 2010).

Parsons, D.J. and S.H. Benedetti. 1979. Impact of fire suppression on a mixed-conifer forest. Forest Ecology and Management 2:21-33.

Pearson, S.F. and D.A. Manuwal. 2001. Breeding bird response to riparian buffer width in managed Pacific Northwest Douglas-fir forests. Ecological Applications 11:840-853.

Raffa, K.F., B.H. Aukema, B.J. Bentz, A.L. Carroll, J.A. Hicke, M.G. Turner , and W.H. Romme. 2008. Cross-scale drivers of natural disturbances prone to anthropogenic amplification: the dynamics of bark beetle eruptions. Bioscience 58:501-517.

Ralph, C.J., G.R. Geupel, P. Pyle, T.E. Martin, and D.F. DeSante. 1993. Handbook of field methods for monitoring landbirds. U.S. Department of Agriculture, Forest Service, Pacific Southwest Research Station, General Technical Report PSW-GTR-144, Albany, California.

Ralph, C.J., P.W.C. Paton, and C.A. Taylor. 1991. Habitat association patterns of breeding birds and small mammals in northwestern California and southwestern Oregon. Pages 379-393 *in* L.F. Ruggiero, K.B. Aubry, A.B. Carey, and M.H. Huff, technical coordinators. Wildlife and vegetation of unmanaged Douglas-fir forests. U.S. Department of Agriculture, Forest Service, Pacific Northwest Research Station , General Technical Report PNW-GTR-285, Portland, Oregon.

Ralph, C.J., J.R. Sauer, and S. Droege, editors. 1995. Monitoring bird populations by point counts. U.S. Department of Agriculture, Forest Service, Pacific Southwest Research Station, General Technical Report PSW-GTR-149, Albany, California.

Raphael, M.G. 2006a. Conservation of the Marbled Murrelet under the Northwest Forest Plan. Conservation Biology 20:297-305.

Raphael, M.G. 2006b. Conservation of listed species: the Northern Spotted Owl and Marbled Murrelet. Pages 16-22 *in* R.W. Haynes, B.T. Bormann, D.C. Lee, and J.R. Martin, editors. The first ten years (1994-2003) of the Northwest Forest Plan: a synthesis of monitoring and research results. U.S. Department of Agriculture, Forest Service, Pacific Northwest Research Station, General Technical Report PNW-GTR-651, Portland, Oregon.

Raphael, M.G., B.G. Marcot., R.S. Holthausen, and M.J. Wisodom. 1998. Interior Columbia Basin Ecosystem Management Program: terrestrial species and habitats. Journal of Forestry 96:22-27.

Raphael, M.G., K.V. Rosenberg, and B.G. Marcot. 1988. Large-scale changes in bird populations of Douglas-fir forests, northwestern California. Bird Conservation 3:63-83.

Reynolds, R.T., J.M. Scott, and R.A. Nussbaum. 1980. A variable circular-plot method for estimating bird numbers. Condor 82:309–313.

Rich, T.D., C.J. Beardmore, H. Berlanga, P.J. Blancher, M.S.W. Bradstreet, G.S. Butcher, D.W. Demarest, E.H. Dunn, W.C. Hunter, E.E. Iñigo-Elias, and others. 2004. Partners in Flight North American landbird conservation plan. Cornell Laboratory of Ornithology, Ithaca, New York.

Rich, T.D., M.J. Wisdom, and V.A. Saab. 2005. Conservation of priority birds in sagebrush ecosystems. U.S. Department of Agriculture, Forest Service, Pacific Southwest Research Station, General Technical Report PSW-GTR-191, Albany, California.

Richardson, T.W. and S.K. Heath. 2005. Effects of conifers on aspen breeding bird communities in the Sierra Nevada. Transactions of the Western Section of the Wildlife Society 40:68-81.

Riparian Habitat Joint Venture. 2004. The riparian bird conservation plan: a strategy for reversing the decline of riparian associated birds in California, v. 2.0. California Partners in Flight, and Point Reyes Bird Observatory, Stinson Beach, California. <http://www.prbo.org/calpif/htmldocs/riparian.html> (23 June 2009).

Ritchie, M.W., and K.A. Harcksen. 1999. Long-term interdisciplinary research on the Goosenest Adaptive Management Area, Klamath National Forest, California. The Forestry Chronicle 75:453-456.

Robertson, B.A., and R.L. Hutto. 2007. Is selectively harvested forest an ecological trap for the Olive-sided Flycatcher? Condor 109:109-121.

Robinson, S.K., F.R. Thompson III, T.M. Donovan, D.R. Whitehead, and J. Faaborg. 1995. Regional forest fragmentation and the nesting success of migratory birds. Science 267:1987-1990.

Root, T.L., J.T. Price, K.R. Hall, S.H. Schneider, C. Rosenzweig, and J.A. Pounds. 2003. Fingerprints of global warming on animals and plants. Nature 421:57-60.

Rose, C.L., B.G. Marcot, T.K. Mellen, J.L. Ohmann, K.L. Wadell, D.L. Lindley, and B. Schreiber. 2001. Decaying wood in Pacific Northwest forests: concepts and tools for habitat management. Pages 580–623 *in* D.H. Johnson., and T.A. O'Neil, managing directors. Wildlife-habitat relationships in Oregon and Washington. Oregon State University Press, Corvallis, Oregon.

Rosenberg, K.V,. and M.G. Raphael. 1986. Effects of forest fragmentation on vertebrates in Douglas-fir forests. Pages 263-272 *in* J. Verner, M.L. Morrison, and C.J. Ralph, editors. Wildlife 2000: modeling habitat relationships of terrestrial vertebrates. University of Wisconsin Press, Madison, Wisconsin.

Rothstein, S.I., and T.L. Cook. 2000. Cowbird management, host population limitation, and efforts to save endangered species: introduction. Pages 323-332 *in* J.N.M. Smith, T.L. Cook, S.I. Rothstein, S.K. Robinson, and S.G. Sealy, editors. Ecology and management of cowbirds and their hosts. University of Texas Press, Austin, Texas.

Ruggiero, L.F., L.L.C. Jones, and K.B. Aubry. 1991. Plant and animal habitat associations in Douglas-fir forests of the Pacific Northwest: an overview. Pages 447-462 *in* L.F. Ruggiero, K.B. Aubry, A.B. Carey, and M.H. Huff, technical coordinators. Wildlife and vegetation of unmanaged Douglas-fir forests. U.S. Department of Agriculture, Forest Service, Pacific Northwest Research Station, General Technical Report PNW-GTR-285, Portland, Oregon.

Saab, V., and H.D.W. Powell. 2005. Fire and avian ecology in North America: process influencing pattern. Studies in Avian Biology 30:1-13.

Sarr, D.A., D.C. Odion, S.R. Mohren, E.E. Perry, R.L. Hoffman, L.K. Bridy, and A.A. Merton. 2007. Vital signs monitoring plan for the Klamath Network: phase III report. U.S. Department of the Interior, National Park Service and Klamath Network Inventory and Monitoring Program. Natural Resource Technical Report NPS/KLMN/NRR-2007/016, Ashland, Oregon. <http://science.nature.nps.gov/im/units/klmn/Monitoring/MON_Phase_III.cfm> (29 April 2010).

Sarr, D., N. Seavy, J. Alexander, and P. Hosten. 2004. Understanding land bird diversity in the Klamath Region. Page 47 *in* Natural Resource Year in Review-2003. U.S. Department of Interior, National Park Service, Washington, D.C.

Sauer, J.R., J.E. Hines, and J. Fallon. 2005. The North American Breeding Bird Survey, results and analysis 1966 – 2005, v. 6.2. <http://www.mbr-pwrc.usgs.gov/bbs/bbs.html> (23 June 2009).

Sauer, J.R., J.E. Hines, and J. Fallon. 2008. The North American Breeding Bird Survey, results and analysis 1966 – 2007, v. 5.15.2008. <http://www.mbr-pwrc.usgs.gov/bbs/bbs.html> (29 April 2010).

Seavy, N.E. 2006. Effects of disturbance on animal communities: fire effects on birds in mixed-conifer forest. Ph.D. dissertation, University of Florida, Gainesville.

Seavy, N.E., J.D. Alexander, and P.E. Hosten. 2008. Bird community composition after mechanical mastication fuel treatments in southwest Oregon oak woodland and chaparral. Forest Ecology and Management 256:774-778.

Sellars, R. 1997. Preserving nature in the National Parks. Yale University Press. New Haven, Connecticut.

Sharp, B.L., and B.E. Kus. 2006. Factors influencing the incidence of cowbird parasitism of Least Bell's Vireos. Journal of Wildlife Management 70:682-690.

Siegel, R.B., and D.F. DeSante. 1999. The draft avian conservation plan forthe Sierra Nevada Bioregion: conservation priorities and strategies for safeguarding Sierra bird populations, v. 1.0. California Partners in Flight, PRBO Conservation Science, and The Institute for Bird Populations, Stinson Beach, California. <http://www.prbo.org/calpif/htmldocs/sierra.html> (23 June 2009).

Sierra Nevada Forest Plan Amendment. 2004. Final Supplemental Environmental Impact Statement and Record of Decision. U.S. Forest Service, Pacific Southwest Region, R5-MB-046. <http://www.fs.fed.us/r5/snfpa/final-seis/> (23 June 2009).

Skinner, C., M.W. Ritchie, T. Hamilton, and J. Symons. 2005. Effects of prescribed fire and thinning on wildlife severity: the Cone fire, Blacks Mountain Experimental Forest. Pages 80-91 *in* Proceedings of the 25th Annual Forest Vegetation Management Conference, January 20-22 2004. Redding, California.

Smith, M.R., P.W. Mattocks, Jr., and K.M. Cassidy. 1997. Breeding birds of Washington State, Volume 4. Pages 137-146 *in* K.M. Cassidy, C.E. Grue, M.R. Smith, and M.K. Dvornich, editors. Washington state Gap analysis – final report. Seattle Audubon Society Publications in Zoology Number 1. Seattle, Washington.

Sperry, J.H., T.L. George, and S. Zack. 2008. Ecological factors affecting response of Dark-eyed Juncos to prescribed burning. Wilson Journal of Ornithology 120:131-138.

Stephens, J.L., and J.D. Alexander. 2006. Association of aspens and bird communities in the Klamath Marsh National Wildlife Refuge: results from bird monitoring, 2003-2005. Unpublished report. Klamath Bird Observatory, Ashland, Oregon.

Stephens, J.L., S.R. Mohren, J.D. Alexander, D.A. Sarr, and K.M. Irvine. 2010. Klamath Network landbird monitoring protocol. U.S. Department of Interior, National Park Service, Natural Resource Report NPS/KLMN/NRR—2010/187, Fort Collins, Colorado.

Stephenson, N.L. 1999. Reference conditions for giant sequoia forest restoration: structure, process, and precision. Ecological Applications 9:1253-1265.

Tappeiner, II, J.C., W.H. Emmingham, and D.E. Hibbs. 2002. Silviculture of Oregon Coast Range forests. Pages 172–190 *in* S.D. Hobbs, J.P. Hayes, R.L. Johnson, G.H. Reeves, T.A. Spies, J.C. Tappeiner II, and G.E. Wells, editors. Forest and stream management in the Oregon Coast Range. Oregon State University Press, Corvallis, Oregon.

Tappeiner, J.C., and J.C. Zasada. 1993. Establishment of salmonberry, salal, vine maple, and bigleaf maple seedlings in the coastal forests of Oregon. Canadian Journal of Forest Research 23:1775–1780.

Tate, K.W. 2005. Long-term environmental effects of conifer removal to achieve aspen release in near stream areas within the northern Sierras. Unpublished report, Lassen National Forest, Susanville, California.

Taylor, A.H. 2000. Fire regimes and forest changes along a montane forest gradient, Lassen Volcanic National Park, southern Cascade Mountains, USA. Journal of Biogeography 27:87-104.

Temple, S.A. and J.A. Wiens. 1989. Bird populations and environmental changes: can birds be bio-indicators? American Birds 43:260-270.

Thomas, J.W., editor. 1979. Wildlife habitats in managed forests: the Blue Mountains of Oregon and Washington. Agriculture Handbook 553. Washington, D.C.

Thomas, J.W., M.G. Raphael, R.G. Anthony, E.D. Forsman, A.G. Gunderson, R.S. Holthausen, B.G. Marcot, G.H. Reeves, J.R. Sedell, and D.M. Solis. 1993. Viability assessments and management considerations for species associated with late-successional and old-growth forests in the Pacific Northwest: the report of the scientific analysis team. U.S. Department of Agriculture, Forest Service, General Technical Report GTR-RM-254, Portland, Oregon.

Thomas, L., J.L. Laake, S. Strindberg, F.F.C. Marques, S.T. Buckland, D.L. Borchers, D.R. Anderson, K.P. Burnham, S.L. Hedley, J.H. Pollard, and others. 2003. Distance 4.1. Research Unit for Wildlife Population Assessment, University of St. Andrews, St. Andrews, United Kingdom. <http://www.ruwpa.st-and.ac.uk/distance/> (16 July 2009).

Thomas, S.C., C.B. Halpern, D.A. Falk, D.A. Liguori, and K.A. Austin. 1999. Plant diversity in managed forests: understory responses to thinning and fertilization. Ecological Applications 9:864–879.

Thysell D.R., and A.B. Carey. 2000. Effects of forest management on understory vegetation: a retrospective study. U.S. Department of Agriculture, Forest Service, Pacific Northwest Research Station, General Technical Report PNW-GTR-488, Olympia, Washington.

Torgersen, T.R., R.R Mason, and R.W. Campbell. 1990. Predation by birds and ants on two forest insect pests in the Pacific Northwest. Studies in Avian Biology 13:14-19.

Trail, P. 2004. Population trends among landbirds of the Klamath-Siskiyou ecoregion: an analysis of breeding bird data. Pages 47-59 in K.L. Mergenthaler, J.E. Williams, and E.S. Jules, editors. Proceedings of the Second Conference on Klamath-Siskiyou Ecology. Siskiyou Field Institute, Cave Junction, Oregon.

U.S. Department of Agriculture and U.S. Department of the Interior. 1994a. Final supplemental environmental impact statement on management of habitat for late-successional and old-growth forest related species within the range of the Northern Spotted Owl. Interagency SEIS Team, Portland, Oregon.

U.S. Department of Agriculture and U.S. Department of the Interior. 1994b. Record of decision for amendments to Forest Service and Bureau of Land Management planning documents within the range of the Northern Spotted Owl and standards and guidelines of management of habitat for late-successional and old-growth forest related species within the range of the Northern Spotted Owl. U.S. Department of Agriculture, Forest Service and U.S. Department of the Interior, Bureau of Land Management, Washington, D.C.

U.S. Fish and Wildlife Service. 1998. Draft recovery plan for the Least Bell's Vireo. U.S. Department of Interior, Fish and Wildlife Service, Pacific Region, Portland, Oregon.

U.S. Fish and Wildlife Service. 1999. Mission Statement. National Policy Issuance #99-01. June 15, 1999. <http://www.fws.gov/policy/npi99_01.html> (8 June 2010).

U.S. Fish and Wildlife Service. 2000. Comprehensive conservation plan for the Little Pend Oreille National Wildlife Refuge. U.S. Department of Interior, Fish and Wildlife Service, Pacific Region, Portland, Oregon. <http://www.fws.gov/pacific/planning/docs/WA/docslpo.htm> (23 June 2009).

U.S. Fish and Wildlife Service. 2003. Klamath Marsh National Wildlife Refuge fire hazard reduction and wildlife habitat enhancement project, final environmental assessment. U.S. Department of Interior, Fish and Wildlife Service, Pacific Region, Portland, Oregon.

U.S. Fish and Wildlife Service. 2005a. Habitat management plan, Little Pend Oreille National Wildlife Refuge. U.S. Department of Interior, Fish and Wildlife Service, Pacific Region, Colville, Washington.

U.S. Fish and Wildlife Service. 2005b. Final comprehensive conservation plan for the Sacramento River National Wildlife Refuge, Sacramento, California. U.S. Department of Interior, Fish and Wildlife Service, Pacific Region, California/Nevada Office, Sacramento, California. <http://www.fws.gov/pacific/planning/draft/docs/CA/docssacriver.htm> (23 June 2009).

U.S. Fish and Wildlife Service. 2005c. Songbird missing from California's Central Valley for 60 years reappears at San Joaquin River National Wildlife Refuge. U.S. Department of Interior, Fish and Wildlife Service, Press Release, Portland, Oregon. <http://www.fws.gov/sacramento/ea/news_releases/2005%20News%20Releases/LBV_rediscover_NR.htm> (23 June 2009).

U.S. Fish and Wildlife Service. 2007. San Joaquin River National Wildlife Refuge Final Comprehensive Conservation Plan. Department of the Interior, U.S. Fish and Wildlife Service, California/Nevada Operations Office, Sacramento, California. <http://www.fws.gov/cno/refuges/sanjoaquin/SJR_CCP_FINAL.pdf> (15 February 2011).

U.S. Fish and Wildlife Service. 2008. Birds of conservation concern 2008. U.S. Department of Interior, Fish and Wildlife Service, Division of Migratory Bird Management, Arlington, Virginia. <http://www.fws.gov/migratorybirds/NewReportsPublications/SpecialTopics/BCC2008/BCC2008.pdf> (6 July 2010).

Vankat, J.L. ,and J. Major. 1978. Vegetation changes in Sequoia National Park, California. Journal of Biogeography 5:377-402.

Vogelmann, J.E., S.M. Howard, L. Yang, C.R. Larson, B.K. Wylie, and J.N. Van Driel. 2001. Completion of the 1990's National Land Cover Data Set for the conterminous United States. Photogrammetric Engineering and Remote Sensing 67:650-662.

Westerling, A.L, H.G. Hidalgo, D.R. Cayan, and T.W. Swetnam. 2006. Warming and earlier spring increase western U.S. forest wildfire activity. Science 313:940-943.

Whitaker, D.M., A.L. Carroll, and W.A. Montevecchi. 2000. Elevated numbers of flying insects and insectivorous birds in riparian buffer strips. Canadian Journal of Zoology 78:740–747.

Williams, B.K., R.C. Szaro, and C.D. Shaprio, C.D. 2009. Adaptive management: the U.S. Department of the Interior technical guide. Adaptive Management Working Group, U.S. Department of the Interior, Washington, D.C.

Zack, S., T.L. George, and W.F. Laudenslayer, Jr. 2002. Are there snags in the system? Comparing "snag-rich" and "snag-poor" eastside pine forests. Pages 179-192 *in* W.F. Laudenslayer, Jr, P.J. Shea, B.E. Valentine, P.C. Weatherspoon, T.E. Lisle, technical coordinators. Proceedings of the symposium on the ecology and management of dead wood in western forests. U.S. Department of Agriculture, Forest Service, Pacific Southwest Research Station, General Technical Report PSW-GTR-181, Albany, California.

Zack, S., W.F. Laudenslayer, T.L. George, C. Skinner, and W. Oliver. 1999. A prospectus on restoring late successional forest structure to eastside in ecosystems through large-scale, interdisciplinary research. Pages 343-355 *in* J. E. Cook and B. P. Oswald, compilers. First biennial North American forest ecology workshop. Forest Ecology Working Group, Society of American Foresters. Raleigh, North Carolina.

Appendix

List of Contributors

John D. Alexander
Klamath Bird Observatory
P.O. Box 758
Ashland, OR 97520
Phone: (541) 201-0866
E-mail: jda@klamathbird.org

Bob Altman
American Bird Conservancy
311 NE Mistletoe Circle
Corvallis, OR 97330
Phone: (541) 745-5339
E-mail: baltman@abcbirds.org

Barb Bresson
U.S. Forest Service
16400 Champion Way
Sandy, OR 97055
Phone: (503) 668-1414
E-mail: bbresson@fs.fed.us

Ryan D. Burnett
PRBO Conservation Science
3820 Cypress Drive #11
Petaluma, CA 94954
Phone: (707) 781-2555
E-mail: rburnett@prbo.org

Daniel Casey
American Bird Conservancy
33 Second St. E
Kalispell, MT 59901
Phone: (406) 756-2681
E-mail: dcasey@abcbirds.org

Susannah Casey
American Bird Conservancy
33 Second St. E
Kalispell, MT 59901
Phone: (406) 756-2681
E-mail: scasey@abcbirds.org

Michael T. Green
U.S. Fish and Wildlife Service
Pacific Region, Division of Migratory Birds &
Habitat Programs
911 NE 11th Ave.
Portland, OR 97232
Phone: (503) 872-2707
E -mail: Michael_Green@fws.gov

Joan C. Hagar
U.S. Geological Service
Biological Resources Discipline, Forest & Rangeland
Ecosystem Science Center
777 NW 9th St., Suite 400
Corvallis, OR 97330
Phone: (541) 758-8815
E-mail: joan_hagar@usgs.gov

Kevin Kilbride
U.S. Fish and Wildlife Service
Pacific Region, Division of Refuges, Columbia River
FPO
1211 SE Cardinal Ct., Suite 100
Vancouver, WA 98683
Phone: (360) 604-2558
E-mail: kevin_kilbride@fws.gov

Kimberly Kreitinger
PRBO Conservation Science
3820 Cypress Drive #11
Petaluma, CA 94954
Phone: (415) 265-9153
E-mail: k.kreitinger@gmail.com

Barbara E. Kus
U.S. Geological Service
Western Ecological Research Center, San Diego
Field Station
4165 Spruance Road, Suite 200
San Diego, CA 92101
Phone: (619) 225-6421
E-mail: barbara_kus@usgs.gov

Sarah McCullough
National Park Service
Klamath Network Inventory and Monitoring
Program
1250 Siskiyou Blvd
Ashland, OR 97520
Phone: (541) 552-8576
E-mail: sarah_mccullough@nps.gov

Nicole L. Michel
Tulane University
Department of Ecology and Evolutionary Biology
400 Boggs Hall
New Orleans, LA 70118
Phone: (504) 261-2942
Email: nmichel@tulane.edu

Sean Mohren
National Park Service
Klamath Network Inventory and Monitoring
Program
1250 Siskiyou Blvd
Ashland, OR 97520
Phone: (541) 552-8576
E-mail: Sean_Mohren@nps.gov

M. Philip Nott
The Institute for Bird Populations
P.O. Box 1346, 11435 State Route 1, Suite 23
Point Reyes Station, CA 94956-1346
Phone: (415) 663-2050
E-mail: pnott@birdpop.org

Fred Paveglio
U.S. Fish and Wildlife Service
Pacific Region, Division of Refuges, Columbia River
FPO
1211 SE Cardinal Ct., Suite 100
Vancouver, WA 98683
Phone: (360) 604-2558
E-mail: fred_paveglio@fws.gov

C. John Ralph
USFS Redwood Sciences Laboratory
1700 Bayview Drive
Arcata, CA 95221
Phone: (707) 825-2992
Email: cjralph@humboldt1.com

Martin G. Raphael
U.S. Forest Service
Pacific Northwest Research Station
3625 93rd Ave SW
Olympia, WA 98512
Phone: (360) 753-7662
E -mail: mraphael@fs.fed.us

Daniel Sarr
National Park Service
Klamath Network Inventory and Monitoring
Program
1250 Siskiyou Blvd
Ashland, OR 97520
Phone: (541) 552-8575
E-mail: Dan_Sarr@nps.gov

Jaime L. Stephens
Klamath Bird Observatory
P.O. Box 758
Ashland, OR 97520
Phone: (541) 201-0866
E-mail: jlh@klamathbird.org

Erin Stockenberg
U.S. Fish and Wildlife Service
911 NE 11th Ave.
Portland, OR 97232
Phone: (503) 231-6840
E-mail: Erin_Stockenberg@fws.gov

Steve Zack
Wildlife Conservation Society
718 SW Alder St., Suite 210
Portland, OR 97205
Phone: (503) 241-3743
E-mail: szack@wcs.org